Know-It-All

Jazz

Know-It-All

Jazz

The 50 Crucial Concepts, Styles & Performers, Each Explained in Under a Minute >

Editor **Dave Gelly**

Contributors

Charles Alexander
Kevin LeGendre
Chris Parker
Brian Priestley
Tony Russell

WELLFLEET PRESS

Brimming with creative inspiration, how-to projects, and useful information to enrich your everyday life, Quarto Knows is a favorite destination for those pursuing their interests and passions. Visit our site and dig deeper with our books into your area of interest: Quarto Creates, Quarto Cooks, Quarto Homes, Quarto Lives, Quarto Drives, Quarto Explores, Quarto Gifts, or Quarto Kids.

Titles are also available at discount for retail,
wholesale, promotional, and bulk purchase.
For details, contact the Special Sales Manager
by email at specialsales@quarto.com
or by mail at The Quarto Group,
Attn: Special Sales Manager,
401 Second Avenue North, Suite 310,
Minneapolis, MN 55401, USA.

10 9 8 7 6 5 4 3 2 1

ISBN: 978-1-57715-175-3

This book was conceived, designed,
and produced by

Ivy Press
An imprint of The Quarto Group
The Old Brewery, 6 Blundell Street
London N7 9BH, United Kingdom
T (0)20 7700 6700 **F** (0)20 7700 8066

Publisher **Susan Kelly**
Creative Director **Michael Whitehead**
Editorial Director **Tom Kitch**
Commissioning Editor **Sophie Collins**
Senior Project Editor **Caroline Earle**
Designer **Ginny Zeal**
Illustrator **Steve Rawlings**
Picture Researcher **Katie Greenwood**
Glossaries Text **Dave Gelly**

Printed in China

MIX
Paper from
responsible sources
FSC® C001701

CONTENTS

INTRODUCTION
Dave Gelly

Jazz was born in the United States at about the same time that sound recording was invented. It was the first form of indigenous popular music able to travel freely beyond its home territory. Before that, only written music had this freedom, and the European classical tradition spread as a result. But most of the world's music is not written down. It is performer's music, not composer's music, and it speaks in its own voices. Arriving when it did, jazz launched its distinctive voice on the world and helped usher in the twentieth century. In the years that followed, it grew, spreading new voices and dialects in luxuriant profusion. This book provides a brief outline of the story so far and shows some directions in which jazz continues to develop.

How This Book Works

We start off with **The Shape of Jazz**, which attempts to answer the question of how jazz works—or, to put it bluntly, how to make out what's going on in a jazz performance. The best guide here is your own ear. If you can honestly say, "I like that," then any information about the item in question should add to your enjoyment and maybe point you toward something else to enjoy.

The history of jazz is like one of those speeded-up movies showing the life of a plant from seed to full flower in a few seconds. Instead of the stately parade of artistic periods—Baroque, classical, romantic, etc.—jazz styles chase each other so quickly that they catch up and even overlap: swing, bebop, hard bop, fusion—it's enough to put any newcomer off. In **Styles of Jazz**, we have pared them down to the barest essentials that still make sense.

As well as understanding the shapes and styles of jazz, it's always useful to know something about the instruments that make it. In **Instruments of Jazz**, we deal with those musical instruments that lend themselves most readily to jazz, although it is theoretically possible to play it on anything—even the bagpipes.

An American art form, *Jazz was invented in the United States, but its appeal soon spread around the world and musicians, such as Louis Armstrong, became global stars.*

Improvisation

The pianist Thelonious Monk was a genius at improvising and is credited as one of the creators of modern jazz and bebop.

The repertoire of more than a century of jazz still rests on two great musical traditions—the Great American Songbook and the blues. Over the years, both have given way slightly in the face of other influences, but they remain major ingredients. Without either of them, jazz as we know it today would not exist. The Songbook is discussed in the chapter on **Vocal Jazz**, while the blues, the "Siamese twin" of jazz, has a chapter— **Jazz & the Blues**—all to itself.

Every form of art, even one as diverse as jazz, has its undisputed classics. In jazz, these take the form of recordings. Our selection in **Classic Jazz Albums** covers half a century—from 1938 to 1989—avoiding the earlier decades, when sound quality might prove a little off-putting, and the later years, when not enough time has elapsed to ensure "classic" status. They are all very well known, but everything is new to someone and their quality is undisputed.

It is impossible to draw a neat line under the story of such a dynamic, evolving art form, and any attempt to foresee the future would be doomed to failure. So in the final chapter, **Today Is the Question**, we leave you with some snapshots from the second decade of the twenty-first century, of an ever-changing, moving target.

Often, the easiest way for jazz lovers to describe the kind of jazz they like is to fire off a list of their favorite artists. In this book, we've kept those names to a minimum by profiling seven of the icons of the genre. You'll also find a short list of 3-Second Biographies accompanying each entry, along with a 3-Second Riff and a 3-Minute Improvisation to provide more information about the topic at a glance.

THE SHAPE OF JAZZ

THE SHAPE OF JAZZ
GLOSSARY

back line A term adopted from rock parlance, this refers to instruments and their players literally at the back of the band—typically drums, bass, guitar, and often piano. The more commonly used jazz term for this is "rhythm section."

bossa nova A sophisticated, urban form of the Brazilian samba, dating from the late 1950s and early 1960s, and much influenced by contemporary American jazz. The idiom was introduced into the United States, notably by Brazilian musicians Antônio Carlos Jobim and João Gilberto and American saxophonist Stan Getz. There was a brief bossa nova craze in 1963–64, which turned Getz into a temporary pop star. The bossa nova rhythm continues to make occasional appearances in jazz to this day.

conservatory A college for advanced musical study; sometimes also called a conservatoire.

Dixieland jazz An early style of jazz first recorded in 1917 by the Original Dixieland Jazz Band and still practiced today, mainly by white musicians.

front line Instruments and their players at the front of a band, such as brass, saxophones, etc.

Great American Songbook The notional name given to the vast body of American popular song composed during the first half of the twentieth century. A good working knowledge of this repertoire was, for many years, vital to every jazz musician. This is not always the case nowadays, but the Songbook is still a massive presence in jazz, not least because many jazz compositions are built on the underlying harmonies of old songs.

Gypsy jazz The style of jazz introduced in the 1930s by the Quintette du Hot Club de France, led by the Gypsy guitarist Django Reinhardt and violinist Stéphane Grappelli. Played almost exclusively on stringed instruments, it now has a worldwide following and is a treasured part of French popular culture. Roma musicians continue to figure among its leading artists.

jam session An informal, unstructured performance by a group of musicians, organized among themselves. Although other people may be present, they are not regarded as an audience. Indeed, the purpose of a jam session is to let musicians play for one another without the distraction of having to entertain nonmusicians. The atmosphere at jam sessions can vary from convivial to highly competitive. A famous example of the latter occurred in 1934, at the Cherry Blossom Club in Kansas City, when Coleman Hawkins is said to have been routed by the cream of the city's tenor saxophonists, including Lester Young. Notable among recorded jam sessions is the series dating from 1953–54 organized around the trombonist Vic Dickenson, where the atmosphere is relaxed and jovial.

ragtime Originally "ragged time," syncopated piano music introduced in the late nineteenth century and regarded as a forerunner of jazz. Its leading figure was Scott Joplin, composer of "The Entertainer," "Maple Leaf Rag," etc. The term later came to mean any lively American popular music, such as Irving Berlin's "Alexander's Ragtime Band."

rhythm section Literally, the instruments and their players generating the "rhythm." Nowadays, it consists almost always of the bass and drums. In prebebop styles, the guitar is generally also present and in preswing styles, the banjo. The piano commonly plays a dual role, acting as part of the rhythm section when accompanying and as a solo instrument at other times.

BANDS, BIG & SMALL

The shapes and sounds of jazz

are so varied that observers can often be baffled by the prospect of defining it. Since the late nineteenth century, the spirit of jazz has surfaced in the sounds of (to name a few) ragtime piano; "trad" or "Dixieland" sextets/septets; harmonized compositions for fifteen- to twenty-piece bands; trios/quartets led by saxophone or trumpet; and bands that look like rock groups but replace the singer with complex instrumental solos. If you look for a common denominator between these highly varied sounds, it's often said the inclusion of improvisation is the answer. But, while this has been key to the establishment of various styles, many of them have become set in their ways—yet they still remain appealing. A defining factor may be that the players' energies are more invested in furthering their own creative contributions and less in pandering to audience expectations. Yet nearly all of these manifestations of jazz were influenced by more popular music and, in turn, have exerted their influence on subsequent pop. Definitions may ultimately be in the mind of the beholder, but it may be comforting (instead of confusing) to note that many of the changes in jazz exist alongside a more popular version of the same style.

3-SECOND RIFF

The abundant changes in how jazz has sounded seem insignificant compared with the energy that fuels it and keeps it distinct from more popular music.

3-MINUTE IMPROVISATION

As in popular-music circles, fashion plays a part in what jazz styles are most accepted at a particular period. But the continuity of tradition is important to jazz players, too, and this can be heard in younger players allied to recent styles repeating (often unconsciously) tunes and phrases from decades earlier. It was this that Miles Davis had in mind when saying, "The history of jazz can be told in four words: Louis Armstrong, Charlie Parker."

RELATED TOPICS

See also

THE DIVERSITY OF STYLES
page 28

CHARLIE PARKER
page 42

LOUIS ARMSTRONG
page 64

MILES DAVIS
page 100

3-SECOND BIOGRAPHIES

LOUIS ARMSTRONG
1901–71
Trumpeter, cornet player, singer, and bandleader

CHARLIE PARKER
1920–55
Alto saxophonist and bandleader

MILES DAVIS
1926–91
Trumpeter, flügelhorn player, and bandleader

EXPERT
Brian Priestley

The size of jazz bands varies as much as the style of music they play.

HOW THE
PARTS FUNCTION

As the styles and sounds of jazz have changed over the decades, the appearance of jazz groups has changed, too. For instance, the professional big bands of the 1930s and 1940s sat in rows and wore uniforms. Jazz-fusion groups in the 1970s, on the other hand, not only dressed like rock musicians but acted like them on stage, too, making it harder for casual observers to notice any regimentation in their actual playing. However, there are certain similarities that come through in the music itself and the way it's organized by the players, and which can link different periods in fairly fundamental ways. There's a broad distinction between the melody instruments—most often, the brass and winds usually described as "horns"—and the rhythm specialists, which include chord instruments and percussionists. The former are the "front line," which may also cover piano or guitar (if there are no horns to take the lead), while the role of the latter, musically and visually, is to form the "back line" or "rhythm section." Despite this perennial distinction in their function, it's a big mistake to think of the melody/front line/lead players as being more important, even if they give that impression, because it's the back line/rhythm section that is crucial in establishing the "feel" or "groove" of a particular piece.

3-SECOND RIFF
No matter what period of jazz you listen to, the difference in function between the rhythm section and the front-line instruments is fundamental.

3-MINUTE IMPROVISATION
While the size of a band's front line is infinitely variable, the rhythm section has become more standardized, almost always including bass and drums and often piano and/or guitar. In earlier times, it was easy for bands to get along without at least one of these components. Drummerless groups were often found, and basses were often missing, because their role was filled by pianists accustomed to playing unaccompanied. But variants are still found today.

RELATED TOPICS
See also
BANDS, BIG & SMALL
page 14

HOW DO THEY KNOW
WHAT TO PLAY?
page 18

EXPERT
Brian Priestley

The melody instruments provide the "front line" while the rhythm instruments form the "back line."

HOW DO THEY KNOW WHAT TO PLAY?

3-SECOND RIFF
Whether the front-line instruments play simultaneously or just one at a time is a reflection of different style periods.

3-MINUTE IMPROVISATION
When groups of musicians say, "What are we going to play?" they probably know each other's styles already. What concerns them is the question of repertoire. Many tunes that are standard in one jazz style are unwelcome in another style of interpretation. Even among the output of the Great American Songbook, some tunes favored in one era then fell out of fashion, while original jazz tunes are usually associated with a single style.

The apparent mystery, for those interested in focusing their jazz listening, is the same mystery for people wanting to learn to play the music—what are jazz musicians doing when they play jazz? The answer is both simple and complex at the same time. Both listeners and would-be players usually begin by being attracted to one style of jazz and, for a while, they identify with that style. They come to understand there are certain things common to different performances in the same style. For instance, the instruments of the rhythm section/back line are filling the same roles and meshing with each other in the same way, whether it's a slow piece or a fast piece. Similarly, the front line/melody instruments may spend long periods playing individually (with backing from the rhythm section) or they may do a lot of working together as an ensemble. These similarities can be seen as constant within that particular style, but the conventions may be in different proportions within another stylistic approach. If it's a style requiring long "solos" with just the rhythm section, the soloists will wait their turn and not intrude on each other's space. If a lot of ensemble playing is the norm, they will learn to blend each other's sounds into a convincing and pleasing whole.

RELATED TOPICS
See also
HOW THE PARTS FUNCTION
page 16

THE DIVERSITY OF STYLES
page 28

GREAT AMERICAN SONGBOOK: THE MEN
page 76

GREAT AMERICAN SONGBOOK: THE WOMEN
page 78

EXPERT
Brian Priestley

Whatever style they play, jazz musicians learn how to blend their instruments together.

THE JAZZ LANGUAGE & HOW IT'S LEARNED

3-SECOND RIFF
The jazz language has been built up over a long period and takes a while for the individual musician to learn.

3-MINUTE IMPROVISATION
What was originally a single language, with an unmistakable American dialect, has spread around the world and been widely imitated, sometimes by non-Americans with an almost flawless accent. But, from the 1930s onward, many musicians in Europe and elsewhere have been less concerned with exact imitation and have learned to make their national music heritage a part of what they bring to the playing of jazz.

Despite the different styles of jazz, there are common factors about the way it sounds, in addition to the basic division of the "sections" (front line and back line). For instance, the role of the drummer remains the same, whenever his or her particular style was developed and, while the drum kit's components have changed and expanded over time, the player's function is to provide a constant energy and appropriate support for the melody instruments. A bassist will fulfill the same role in another way, giving a solid and stimulating lift to the front-line members. The latter players will draw on a vocabulary assembled over the decades by their predecessors, as well as making their own distinctive additions as they go along. How this vocabulary is picked up is partly intuitive but also requires years of formal or informal study. The method used to be: learn your instrument well enough to get gigs with local bands; pick up ideas from more experienced musicians; and, after gaining sufficient confidence, "sit in" at jam sessions. These avenues are less available now, because jazz has diverged from more popular styles, and players today will often start with pop music and then migrate toward jazz. But those who identify with jazz at an early age can now find a wide range of speciality courses at colleges and conservatories.

RELATED TOPICS
See also
HOW DO THEY KNOW WHAT TO PLAY?
page 18

EUROPEAN JAZZ
page 48

CITIZENS OF THE WORLD
page 136

EXPERT
Brian Priestley

Musicians from around the world have learned the "language" of American jazz.

1899
Born in Washington, D.C., as Edward Kennedy Ellington; he earned the nickname "Duke" at an early age due to his aristocratic demeanor

1917
Starts providing function bands, featuring his piano

1923
First visits New York, inheriting leadership of The Washingtonians group

1927
Becomes the resident bandleader at Harlem's Cotton Club

1933
After touring the United States, his first tour of Europe encourages his compositional ambition

1943
Performs his first concert at Carnegie Hall

1956
His appearance at the open-air Newport Festival boosts his audiences and foreign tours

1965
Introduces "sacred concerts" at San Francisco's Grace Cathedral

1974
Dies in New York City

DUKE ELLINGTON

Most of the key individuals in

jazz have been trumpeters or reedplayers such as saxophonists and clarinetists. Duke Ellington was unusual in exerting wide influence, despite sitting at the piano or conducting his band. Initially considered just one of many such leaders, he achieved a unique manner of cultivating his bandmembers' talents and combining their contributions into a satisfying whole.

By 1899, Washington, D.C., had a large percentage of middle-class African-Americans, and Ellington's relatively privileged upbringing fed his ambitions in both music and fine art, for which he won a scholarship to study in Brooklyn. Turning it down in favor of the piano and putting together casual bands, he eventually moved to New York City with local bandleader Elmer Snowden, whose group, The Washingtonians, deposed their leader and elected Ellington in his place.

Becoming skilled at exploiting his sidemen's skills, Ellington's growth as a composer and arranger was beneficially forced by becoming resident at Harlem's Cotton Club. This required a constant stream of original material for dance routines and provided a stable venue for late-night experimental rehearsals. His most distinctive 1920s soloist, trumpeter Bubber Miley, was followed by such individualistic figures as Cootie Williams and Rex Stewart, and saxophonists Johnny Hodges and Ben Webster.

Deploying their sounds in short features, he also used his Carnegie Hall appearances of the 1940s to premiere extended compositions, such as "Black, Brown and Beige" and "The Tattooed Bride." But his charismatic persona enabled him to cultivate audiences for both "serious" works and populist rhythmic extravaganzas. His Newport Festival version of "Diminuendo and Crescendo in Blue" combined both extremes in a single 14-minute piece.

His earlier pop hits such as "Mood Indigo," "Solitude," and "In A Sentimental Mood," provided sufficient royalties to subsidize the continuance of his band into the 1970s. An affinity for song also fed into the vocal-dominated Sacred Concerts that engendered much of the original music of Ellington's last decade.

Brian Priestley

WHERE JAZZ WAS PLAYED IN THE PAST

3-SECOND RIFF

Jazz was born in the United States, but, thanks to the invention of sound recording and then radio, it soon spread around the world.

3-MINUTE IMPROVISATION

As with classical composers, many jazz performers benefited from the demands and the largesse of benefactors. The gangsters who ran America's illegal alcohol industry in the 1920s, and drugs supply chains from the 1940s on, found it helpful to own nightclubs that needed to employ musicians. Since then, jazz-appreciation societies, all-purpose concert halls, educational establishments, and even official subsidized funding bodies have all played their part in helping the music to be heard.

Jam sessions were the college courses of yesteryear, commonly taking place late at night, after the paying customers for more popular music had left the dance hall or nightclub. Some venues also provided straight jazz for their patrons, and specialty clubs still do. This branch of the entertainment business, which grew up in the United States in the early twentieth century, spread rapidly to Europe, Asia, and the southern hemisphere. After jazz began to be documented in recording studios from the late 1910s, again initially in the United States, it rapidly invaded radio stations and private living rooms around the world. However, its most vibrant expressions—and most of its stylistic changes—were usually incubated in local communities, especially ones with significant African-American populations. New Orleans in the 1910s, Chicago in the 1920s, Kansas City in the 1930s, and New York throughout this period never had a monopoly on the playing of jazz, but they did provide the hothouse atmosphere in which sufficient numbers of musicians could thrive. Although many American jazz players went to Europe during this time, it was only gradually that local musicians began to successfully emulate them. From the 1930s on, the idea of celebrating jazz as an art and forming specialty appreciation societies took root, especially in Europe.

RELATED TOPICS

See also
WHERE JAZZ IS PLAYED NOW
page 26

EUROPEAN JAZZ
page 48

EXPERT
Brian Priestley

The advent of sound recording and radio spread the appeal of jazz beyond the nightclubs.

WHERE JAZZ
IS PLAYED NOW

3-SECOND RIFF
Not only is jazz now played worldwide, but the type of live venues also continues to expand, and the Internet makes it available as never before.

3-MINUTE IMPROVISATION
In addition to the high-profile commercial and subsidized outlets, jazz still finds a place in local bars and cafés and even at functions in private homes. But it's worth noting that the majority of private listening has taken place without the presence of live musicians. The availability of records and tapes (and now computers or phones) has made it possible to listen after the music has been performed live.

Geographically, the spread of jazz has continued to widen. Countries that suffered in World War II, such as Japan and several European states, embraced jazz and the way it is performed as a symbol of democracy and freedom and included it in their cultural subsidies. As a commercial enterprise, the music benefited from increasing status, symbolized by large outdoor festivals, such as those in Newport and Montreal, and international tours of concert halls. Jazz continues to be the subject of both innovation and stylistic consolidation, and each of these approaches is more accepted than ever before. The locations in which jazz is played are also expanding—not only festivals and concert halls but also dance clubs, colleges, and community venues. In addition, the vast library of recorded jazz is more easily accessed via the Internet, and it is being augmented by the discovery of long-lost video material. Some of the long-established jazz clubs are even making their live presentations available through live streaming. While these manifestations make it easier for musicians to be heard and seen at minimal expense, it becomes harder for anyone other than big-name players to earn a decent income from their music. But there still seems no shortage of people willing to try.

RELATED TOPICS
See also
WHERE JAZZ WAS PLAYED
IN THE PAST
page 24

CITIZENS OF THE WORLD
page 136

EXPERT
Brian Priestley

As well as live performances at clubs and festivals, recorded jazz is now more accessible than ever before.

THE DIVERSITY OF STYLES

3-SECOND RIFF

Jazz has gone through a number of stylistic revisions but has benefited enormously from its ability to change and absorb outside influences.

3-MINUTE IMPROVISATION

The arrival of recording in the early twentieth century made it easier for musicians to assimilate what others were doing and to find out how to develop and extend it. It also brought about the situation where all the music, whether made yesterday or 100 years ago, is not only available for the listener but also for the up-and-coming musician to choose an early style or to combine elements that originally seemed incompatible.

The stylistic diversity of jazz should be seen as one of its most attractive (and most vibrant) features, instead of as a barrier to its appreciation. Improvisation may be less fundamental to jazz than it's often believed to be, but it certainly exists as an element within all the different stylistic conventions and may indeed have helped in their creation. The geographical spread of the music has also been the cause of several distinctive variations: examples include the so-called "Gypsy jazz" that came together in Europe in the 1930s but is now equally popular in American jazz circles. You could also include here the "bossa nova," a term originally applied to a style of Brazilian popular song from the late 1950s onward, which mixed a particularly laid-back samba rhythm with jazz-influenced harmonies and, eventually, instrumental improvisation. Once you get used to the existence of different styles and begin to understand the mechanics of some of them, it becomes easier to understand other styles. Gradually, you realize how the styles relate to each other historically, and you begin to appreciate that the shape-shifting nature of the jazz impulse is one of its greatest strengths.

RELATED TOPICS

See also
HOW DO THEY KNOW WHAT TO PLAY?
page 18

THE JAZZ LANGUAGE & HOW IT'S LEARNED
page 20

BOSSA NOVA TO FREEDOM
page 44

EUROPEAN JAZZ
page 48

EXPERT
Brian Priestley

"Calypso King of New York" Wilmoth Houdini, guitarist Django Reinhardt, violinist Stuff Smith, and bandleader Stan Kenton illustrate the variety of backgrounds brought to the creation of jazz.

STYLES OF JAZZ

STYLES OF JAZZ
GLOSSARY

big band Normally a band of around sixteen players, arranged in sections—trumpets, trombones, saxophones, rhythm. This format evolved in the late 1920s and early 1930s as the standard American dance orchestra, reaching its apotheosis in the swing era of the late 1930s. Big bands for dancing declined in popularity after World War II, but a few of those with a jazz reputation survived or soon reformed—notably those of Count Basie, Duke Ellington, and Woody Herman. They now played mainly to concert audiences and were joined by others, such as Stan Kenton's orchestra and the Gerry Mulligan Concert Band. In more recent times, the standard big-band formula has grown somewhat stiff and predictable, relying on complex arrangements and virtuosic ensemble playing.

Dixieland jazz An early style of jazz first recorded in 1917 by the Original Dixieland Jazz Band and still practiced today, mainly by white musicians.

ensemble Instruments playing together, as opposed to solo.

front line Instruments and their players at the front of a band, such as brass, saxophones, etc.

jump band Originally, any small improvising band. Now the term usually refers to a small, entertaining show band playing for dancing in the revived 1940s style known as "Lindy Hop" or "Jitterbug." This style of music is sometimes called "Jump 'n' Jive."

modal jazz Jazz based on "modes" or nonstandard scales, as opposed to the resolving chromatic harmonies of standard popular songs.

polyrhythm Two or more rhythms played simultaneously.

Prohibition The period between 1920 and 1933 when, following the 18th Amendment to the U.S. Constitution, the supply and consumption of alcohol was illegal in the United States. The result was an explosive growth of illegal drinking, facilitated with great efficiency by the criminal underworld. Jazz, especially in New York, Chicago, and Kansas City, was a happy beneficiary. See also speakeasy.

R&B Short for "rhythm and blues," the description applied in some U.S. record catalogs to products aimed at African-American buyers. The term came to be applied to the genre of black music that preceded rock 'n' roll.

ragtime Originally "ragged time," or syncopated piano music introduced in the late nineteenth century and regarded as a forerunner of jazz. Its leading figure was Scott Joplin, composer of "The Entertainer," "Maple Leaf Rag," etc. The term later came to mean any lively American popular music, such as Irving Berlin's "Alexander's Ragtime Band."

rhythm section Literally, the instruments and their players generating the "rhythm". Nowadays it consists almost always of the bass and drums. In prebebop styles, the guitar is generally also present and in preswing styles, the banjo. The piano commonly plays a dual role, acting as part of the rhythm section when accompanying and as a solo instrument at other times.

speakeasy A type of illegal drinking establishment that flourished in the United States during Prohibition.

Storyville The notorious "red light" district of New Orleans, where jazz pioneers such as Jelly Roll Morton worked. It was forcibly shut down by the U.S. Navy in 1917.

third stream A hybrid form containing elements of both jazz and European classical music.

timbre Instrumental or vocal tone.

NEW ORLEANS & CLASSIC JAZZ

3-SECOND RIFF

Fresh and exuberant but tinged with sadness, classic jazz, with its emphasis on spontaneous ensemble interaction and rhythmic buoyancy, laid the foundations for swing, bebop, and post-bop jazz.

3-MINUTE IMPROVISATION

Beginning as a strictly ensemble-based music, classic jazz swiftly produced solo stars, such as trumpet/cornet players Louis Armstrong, Henry "Red" Allen, and Bix Beiderbecke; clarinet player/soprano saxophonist Sidney Bechet; and composer/pianist Jelly Roll Morton. Such figures brought new textural (and emotional) possibilities to jazz, so that the music was later able to accommodate, via swing bands, both a rhythmic base for dancers and also highly personal solo statements that rewarded repeated close listening.

Although the seeds of jazz—West African rhythms mixed with European, local folk, and religious music—sprang up into improvised music (ragtime) from Texas to Baltimore, New Orleans provided the music's most fertile soil. A port city and a melting pot of African, West Indian, and French culture, New Orleans was steeped in music, from its red-light district, known as Storyville, to its funerals and parades. Its local musicians pioneered an extrovert but surprisingly subtle and emotionally complex style of spontaneous, collective improvisation. This was spearheaded by the trumpet/cornet playing of the likes of Buddy Bolden and Freddie Keppard, decorated by sinuous clarinet and sonorous trombone to form the classic three-horn front line, and driven by a rhythm section comprising guitar/banjo, bass (initially brass, but later string), piano, and drums. The closing of Storyville in 1917 encouraged musicians to migrate to Chicago, Kansas City, and New York, with bandleaders such as Joe "King" Oliver and his protégé Louis Armstrong disseminating New Orleans music in the process. In the same year, the Original Dixieland Jazz Band made the first jazz record, preparing the ground for 1920s classic jazz recordings, from the large-ensemble, arranged music of Jelly Roll Morton and his Red Hot Peppers to the punchier, small-ensemble music of Armstrong's Hot Five/Seven.

RELATED TOPICS

See also
SWING
page 36

BEBOP TO HARD BOP
page 40

LOUIS ARMSTRONG
page 64

3-SECOND BIOGRAPHIES

JOE "KING" OLIVER
1885–1938
Cornet player, composer, and bandleader

FREDDIE KEPPARD
1890–1933
Cornet player with Original Creole Orchestra

JELLY ROLL MORTON
1890–1941
Pianist, vocalist, composer, and arranger

EXPERT
Chris Parker

"Peanuts" Hucko (clarinet), Louis Armstrong (trumpet), Jack Teagarden (trombone): a classic New Orleans front line.

SWING

As jazz spread across the United States, it added virtuosic soloing skills and increased musical complexity (summed up in "swing," denoting a tension between a regular rhythm-section pulse and subtle variations provided by the band's front line) to its core value of lively ensemble interactiveness. The recruitment, in 1924, of New Orleans musician par excellence Louis Armstrong and of Coleman Hawkins, a musician playing what had hitherto been regarded as an "illegitimate" jazz instrument, the saxophone, into the large unit run in New York by Fletcher Henderson epitomized this transition. Big bands ranged from those adhering relatively closely to the New Orleans spirit, such as the ten-piece Luis Russell band, through buoyant blues-based units, such as Bennie Moten's, to the arranged sophistication of Henderson's band and also that of Duke Ellington. Urban entertainment venues, such as New York's Savoy Ballroom and Cotton Club, provided work for such bands, and the speakeasy culture which sprang up during Prohibition also helped prepare the ground for wide public acceptance of more commercially oriented soloists/bandleaders, such as Benny Goodman, Artie Shaw, and Glenn Miller, whose big-band sound, in the decade between the mid-1930s and mid-1940s, became America's popular music.

3-SECOND RIFF

Swing's essence is distilled in Duke Ellington's 1931 composition "It Don't Mean a Thing (If It Ain't Got That Swing)."

3-MINUTE IMPROVISATION

Swing was also purveyed by small groups, such as those employed on "Swing Street" (New York's 52nd Street) in the late 1930s and early 1940s. These bands laid the foundations for mainstream jazz in the 1950s, which (in the main) eschewed the concentration on polyrhythms, chordal extensions, and the nervy angularity characterizing bebop.

RELATED TOPICS

See also
DUKE ELLINGTON
page 22

ORCHESTRAL JAZZ
page 38

BEBOP TO HARD BOP
page 40

3-SECOND BIOGRAPHIES

FLETCHER HENDERSON
1897–1952
Pianist, arranger, and composer

LUIS RUSSELL
1902–63
Brought New Orleans musicians into larger-ensemble jazz

COLEMAN HAWKINS
1904–69
Chief creator of saxophone's jazz vocabulary

EXPERT

Chris Parker

Benny Goodman, the "King of Swing", and Coleman Hawkins (inset) were key figures in the swing era.

ORCHESTRAL JAZZ

3-SECOND RIFF
Celebrated guitarist/
raconteur/man about jazz
Eddie Condon poured scorn
on Whiteman for "trying to
make a lady out of jazz."

**3-MINUTE
IMPROVISATION**
Many feel that orchestral
jazz can be somewhat
stuffy and stultifying, but
it laid the foundations for
such universally admired
figures as Gil Evans and
Miles Davis (*Sketches of
Spain*, *Porgy and Bess*) and
Duke Ellington and Charles
Mingus, whose extended
compositions drew
inspiration from the
ambitiousness of
symphonic jazz.

The term "orchestral jazz" can
refer to any of the structurally sophisticated
arranged music played by large aggregations,
but it more properly denotes music utilizing
string and woodwind sections in addition to the
jazz big band's brass, saxophones, and four- or
five-piece rhythm section. The pioneer of such
music was Paul Whiteman, self-styled "King of
Jazz." He employed the cream of contemporary
players (trumpeter Bix Beiderbecke, violinist Joe
Venuti, and saxophonist Frankie Trumbauer
chief among them) to play music ranging from
polished, somewhat polite but consistently lively
jazz to more complex compositions drawing on
the classical tradition, most famously George
Gershwin's "Rhapsody in Blue," still America's
most popular concert work. Orchestrated jazz
reemerged sporadically throughout the music's
history, most famously in Stan Kenton's 1953
album of Bob Graettinger compositions, *City of
Glass*. It also manifested itself in small-group
settings (most successfully in Stan Getz's *Focus*,
arranged and composed by Eddie Sauter, and
also—with more mixed results—in Charlie Parker's
recordings with strings), but the form has always
been regarded with mild suspicion by hardcore
jazz aficionados, despite a brief renaissance in
the 1950s with "third stream" music.

RELATED TOPICS
See also
DUKE ELLINGTON
page 22

SWING
page 36

3-SECOND BIOGRAPHIES
PAUL WHITEMAN
1890–1967
Bandleader and violinist

GEORGE GERSHWIN
1898–1937
Pianist, composer,
and songwriter

EDDIE SAUTER
1914–1981
Arranger and composer

EXPERT
Chris Parker

*Jazz has always been
hospitable to ambitious,
structured compositions,
from the timeless
classics of George
Gershwin (center) to
the trailblazing
big-band adventures
of Stan Kenton.*

BEBOP TO HARD BOP

In the early 1940s, many jazz musicians fretted about the artistic restrictions placed on them by the increasingly formulaic nature of big-band jazz. Exploring the musical ideas of trumpeter Dizzy Gillespie, drummer Kenny Clarke and pianist/composer Thelonious Monk at jam sessions in New York clubs, such as Minton's and Monroe's, a growing coterie of like-minded players forged a new style of jazz, initially called bebop (for onomatopoeic reasons), later shortened to bop. Stripping tunes down to their chordal bases and playing at forbidding tempos, soloists such as Charlie Parker (alto), Charlie Christian (guitar), and Gillespie himself, created a virtuosic, nervily frenetic, often fiercely joyous sound emphasizing artistic individuality and originality, in the process rendering the music more hospitable to polyrhythms and harmonic adventurousness. These musical qualities eventually permeated the jazz world, filtering through into the late-1950s style known as hard bop, which simplified bebop's somewhat esoteric complexity by drawing on the more straightforward expressiveness of R&B and 1930s jump bands to produce infectiously rhythmic music whose vibrant accessibility continues to attract new listeners to jazz (via classic recordings by the likes of Art Blakey, Horace Silver, and Lee Morgan) to this day.

RELATED TOPICS
See also
NEW ORLEANS
& CLASSIC JAZZ
page 34

SWING
page 36

CHARLIE PARKER
page 42

3-SECOND BIOGRAPHIES
THELONIOUS MONK
1917–82
Pianist, composer,
and musical guru

DIZZY GILLESPIE
1917–93
Trumpeter, composer, and
indefatigable sparkplug

ART BLAKEY
1919–90
Drummer and bandleader

EXPERT
Chris Parker

Dizzy Gillespie, Charlie Parker, Miles Davis (left to right)—three towering figures in the creation of small-group jazz.

1920
Born in Kansas City,
Missouri

1936–42
Plays in local bands run
by the likes of Tommy
Douglas and Buster
Smith before joining
Jay McShann; he is also
strongly influenced by
trumpeter Roy Eldridge,
virtuoso pianist Art
Iatum, and guitarist
Biddy Fleet

1942–44
Big-band work with Earl
Hines and Billy Eckstine

1944–45
Small-group work on
New York's 52nd Street.
Savoy recordings of bebop
staples such as "Now's
the Time," "Ko-Ko," and
"Billie's Bounce" alongside
Gillespie, Davis, bassist
Curley Russell, and
drummer Max Roach

1946–47
Stays on West Coast,
hospitalized for six
months due to his
heroin addiction

1949
Makes European debut
at the Paris International
Jazz Festival, followed by
a visit to Scandinavia the
following year

1950
The height of his
career as a soloist, his
recordings with strings
were popular

1950–55
Gigs around United
States with local bands,
to his increasing
frustration

1955
Dies in apartment of
Baroness Pannonica
de Koenigswater

CHARLIE PARKER

Often cited as the most extravagantly gifted improviser in the history of jazz (although Louis Armstrong, Coleman Hawkins, and John Coltrane are also strong candidates for this title), alto saxophonist Charlie Parker, known to contemporaries as "Bird," was one of the pioneers of bebop and a crucially important figure in the development of modern jazz.

After cutting his teeth in the blues-based band of pianist Jay McShann in his hometown of Kansas City, Parker followed in the footsteps of jazz itself by moving north, initially (and briefly) to Chicago, and then (permanently) to New York in 1941. Having established himself in the jazz capital, with the help of his musical mentor Buster Smith, Parker—along with his front line partners, including trumpeters Dizzy Gillespie and Miles Davis—oversaw the music's transition from swing (accessible, danceable, usually played by big bands) to bebop (esoteric, often frenetically nervy small-group music). Although pianist/composer Thelonious Monk and Gillespie were the chief musical theorists of this movement, Parker, according to drummer Max Roach, "had a great mathematical mind, where he measured notes and could spin off profound thought musically."

Like a figure many see as his rock equivalent, Jimi Hendrix, Parker, despite his much-publicized and ultimately fatal predilection for self-medication, was a profoundly serious and thoughtful artist, obsessed with musical innovation and virtuosity. By the 1950s (courtesy of numerous recordings—some featuring his searing alto jostling with a conventional jazz front line, others with strings—and tireless gigging), he had established himself as the most influential soloist in jazz. His apparently effortless, protean inventiveness, both harmonic and rhythmic, laid the groundwork for all jazz's subsequent progress, from hard bop through modal jazz to free form, and his wildly exuberant, fiercely joyous small-group sides, especially those featuring Gillespie and Roach, are among the most exhilarating recordings made in the twentieth century.

On Parker's shockingly premature death in 1955, "Bird Lives!" immediately appeared on walls in New York; his spirit will certainly live on as long as jazz is played.

Chris Parker

BOSSA NOVA
TO FREEDOM

3-SECOND RIFF
Although it was a relatively
short-lived craze, bossa
nova had lasting appeal,
and mainstream jazz
musicians still regularly
include this style in their
concert repertoires.

**3-MINUTE
IMPROVISATION**
Free jazz, while sharing
the artistic aims of free
verse (liberation from the
"tyranny" of regular meter,
rhyme/harmony, and
overall predetermined
structure), also attracted
similar criticism, summed
up by Robert Frost's
description of *vers libre* as
"tennis without a net."

In the 1960s, while cutting-edge
jazz continued to explore various routes toward
freedom, the form also spawned a musical
"craze," bossa nova. Imbued with the laid-back
warmth associated with West Coast jazz, and
inspired by Brazilian maestros João Gilberto and
Luiz Bonfá, the likes of tenor player Stan Getz
and guitarist Charlie Byrd produced a beguiling
mix of soft Latin waft and jazz improvisation.
Free jazz, however, took the pioneering abstract
musical experiments of pianist Lennie Tristano,
the bluesy melodic improvisation of saxophonist
Ornette Coleman, and the torrential unfettered
piano playing of Cecil Taylor and forged a music
relying on spontaneous improvisation rather
than on predetermined structures, harmonic or
metrical. While American free-jazz artists, such
as Archie Shepp, John Coltrane, and Albert Ayler,
demanded political as well as artistic freedom,
European free improvisers such as Joe Harriott,
Derek Bailey, and Evan Parker, aspired towards
total abstraction, providing jazz with a greatly
enriched vocabulary of textures and timbres in
the process. By the end of the 1960s, however,
many exponents had returned to more structured
music, and Miles Davis (whose 1959 "modal"
album *Kind of Blue*, with its reliance on scales
instead of chord sequences, had opened up
possibilities for free jazz) was pioneering electric
"fusion" music.

RELATED TOPICS
See also
THE JAZZ LANGUAGE
& HOW IT'S LEARNED
page 20

BEBOP TO HARD BOP
page 40

CITIZENS OF THE WORLD
page 136

3-SECOND BIOGRAPHIES
JOHN COLTRANE
1926–67
Leading "modal" saxophonist,
uniquely influential and
inspirational figure

ORNETTE COLEMAN
1930–2015
Composer, theorist,
and saxophonist

ARCHIE SHEPP
1937–
Composer, educator,
and saxophonist

EXPERT
Chris Parker

*In the 1960s, jazz
accommodated both
abstract free jazz and
the gentle waft of
bossa nova.*

JAZZ ROCK & FUSION

3-SECOND RIFF

Pioneered by Miles Davis, jazz rock/fusion brought elements of both rock and world music into jazz. It was a combination that has proved to have a lasting appeal.

3-MINUTE IMPROVISATION

The musical validity of jazz rock/fusion was born out by its fecundity and longevity. By the 1980s, even ostensibly die-hard acoustic musicians, such as Jimmy Giuffre, were leading fusion bands, and numerous big bands featured electric bassists and lengthy, head-banging guitar solos. In the new millennium, fusion is merely another readily accepted branch of the music.

Like Kansas City in *Oklahoma!*, jazz musicians had "gone about as fur as they can go" in the late 1960s, hemorrhaging audience numbers in the process, so Miles Davis's move into jazz rock or fusion was initially greeted with cynicism in some circles. The form's immediate popularity, however—and its ready accommodation of vibrant new textures, sounds, and rhythms—resulted in something of a renaissance for the music. Davis's bands spawned a plethora of innovative jazz fusion from former sidemen, including keyboard players Chick Corea (Return to Forever) and Herbie Hancock (The Headhunters), guitarist John McLaughlin (Mahavishnu Orchestra), and keyboardist Joe Zawinul and saxophonist Wayne Shorter (Weather Report). Guitarist Larry Coryell was also influential with Free Spirits, and in Europe bands, such as Ian Carr's Nucleus, and big-band leaders (Mike Westbrook and Mike Gibbs among them) allowed rock influences into their music. Jazz and rock both had roots in blues and R&B, so the arrival of a new generation of jazz musicians who had grown up listening to rock (and—guitarists in particular—playing with blues organists, such as Jimmy Smith) made the transition into fusion a natural one for many, and by the 1980s, rock rhythms and textures were thoroughly assimilated into the jazz mainstream.

RELATED TOPICS

See also
EUROPEAN JAZZ
page 48

GUITAR
page 68

MILES DAVIS
page 100

3-SECOND BIOGRAPHIES

HERBIE HANCOCK
1940–
Pianist and composer

CHICK COREA
1941–
Pianist and composer

JOHN MCLAUGHLIN
1942–
Guitarist and fusion/world-music pioneer

EXPERT
Chris Parker

Jazz has embraced all manner of electronic instruments usually associated with rock, from bass guitars to Fender Rhodes pianos.

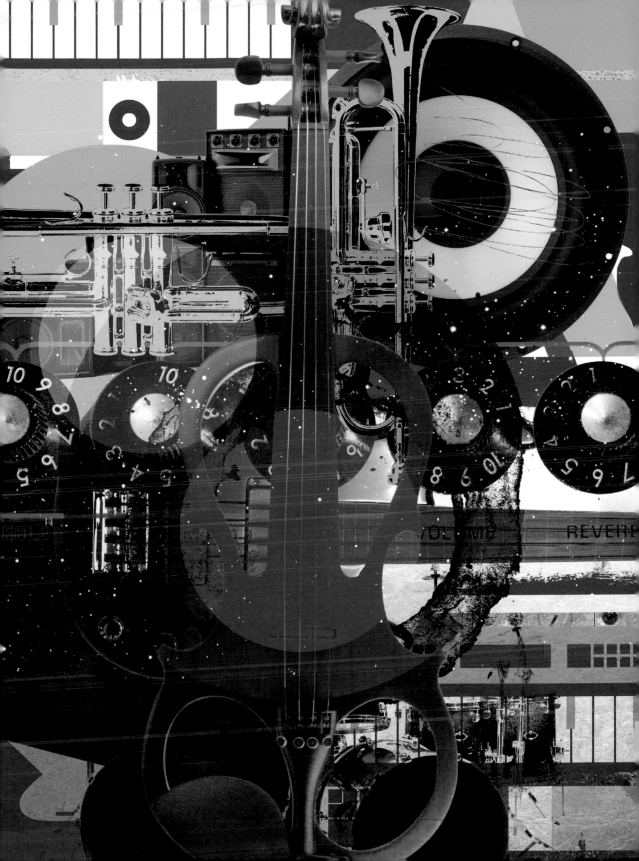

EUROPEAN JAZZ

3-SECOND RIFF
Many observers trace "European" jazz to the modal innovations of Miles Davis's *Kind of Blue*, which replaced a reliance on the chord sequences of popular song with an approach more akin to that of folk music.

3-MINUTE IMPROVISATION
Roman mayor Walter Veltroni, after authorizing a subsidy of about 6.8 million dollars for a city-center "Casa del Jazz," rebutted charges of sponsoring U.S. cultural imperialism thus: "Jazz has become a global language. It may be American in origin, but it has been absorbing different influences, including Italian. Jazz belongs to all the world now."

While Europe has always been in the vanguard as far as jazz appreciation is concerned (providing the form's first book-length study, the first jazz magazine, and the first discography), the continent has produced recognizably "European" jazz only relatively recently. Belgian-born guitarist Django Reinhardt produced identifiably "local" music in the 1930s and 1940s, and UK composers such as Stan Tracey (1965's pioneering *Under Milk Wood*), Michael Garrick, Mike Westbrook, and Neil Ardley, all produced unmistakably European music from the 1960s onward. In the 1970s, the German label ECM began documenting home-grown music with a scrupulous attention to sound quality more readily associated with classical recordings. Saxophonists/composers such as Jan Garbarek (Norway), Carlo Actis Dato (Italy), John Surman (UK), and Louis Sclavis (France) produced jazz firmly rooted both in indigenous folk and popular traditions; countries with vibrant immigrant-based musical traditions (such as reggae in the UK and Maghrebi music in France), stirred these influences into the pot, and the result, in the new millennium, jazz is as likely to be sparked by Sami yoiks (Scandinavia) or Moravian folk music (Czech Republic) as by swing or hard bop.

RELATED TOPICS
See also
WHERE JAZZ IS PLAYED NOW
page 26

THE DIVERSITY OF STYLES
page 28

CITIZENS OF THE WORLD
page 136

3-SECOND BIOGRAPHIES
DJANGO REINHARDT
1910–53
Virtuoso guitarist, the first world-famous European jazz musician

STAN TRACEY
1926–2013
British pianist and composer

JAN GARBAREK
1947–
Norwegian soprano/tenor saxophonist and eclectic composer

EXPERT
Chris Parker

Jazz based in European culture incorporates, instead of being subservient to, American influences.

INSTRUMENTS OF JAZZ

INSTRUMENTS OF JAZZ
GLOSSARY

alto saxophone See saxophone

back line A term adopted from rock parlance, this refers to instruments and their players literally at the back of the band—typically drums, bass, guitar, and often piano. The more usual jazz term for this is "rhythm section."

baritone saxophone See saxophone

conga Tall Afro-Cuban drum, played by the fingers and hollowed palm of the hand.

front line Instruments and their players at the front of a band, such as brass, saxophones, etc.

Gypsy jazz The style of jazz introduced in the 1930s by the Quintette du Hot Club de France, led by the Gypsy guitarist Django Reinhardt and violinist Stéphane Grappelli. Played almost exclusively on stringed instruments, it now has a worldwide following and is a treasured part of French popular culture.

Latin jazz Jazz based on Latin-American rhythms in place of the more customary jazz beat. These rhythms are often played by a number of percussion instruments, each repeating a simple pattern. The Spanish habañera rhythm, ubiquitous in the Caribbean region, remains an essential ingredient of New Orleans street music to this day.

mute Device for altering the sound of brass instruments. Placed inside or in front of the instrument's bell, a mute interferes with the passage of sound, thereby suppressing or distorting it. Jazz trumpeters and trombonists can he heard playing a large variety of mutes, although some do not use them at all.

reed section The saxophone section of a big band, whose members play additional reed instruments such as the clarinet.

rhythm section Literally, the instruments and their players generating the "rhythm." Nowadays, it consists almost always of the bass and drums. In prebebop styles, the guitar is generally also present and in preswing styles the banjo. The piano commonly plays a dual role, acting as part of the rhythm section when accompanying and as a solo instrument at other times.

saxophone The emblematic jazz instrument. Although made of brass, it is in fact a woodwind instrument, its sound generated by a vibrating reed attached to a clarinet-type mouthpiece. The saxophone is actually a family of instruments of differing sizes and pitches. The most common nowadays are the four that roughly correspond to the pitches of choral singing: soprano, alto, tenor, and baritone. There is a considerable overlap in their ranges, allowing them to blend seamlessly into a saxophone section. It has often been remarked that the sound of the saxophone bears an uncanny resemblance to the human voice, and, as with the human voice, no two players' tones are exactly alike. The soprano, which is not normally in a J shape but straight, like a clarinet, was relatively rare until the 1960s. It owes its popularity to John Coltrane, who took it up to supplement his use of the tenor. It is not a regular member of the saxophone section. The alto is often the first choice of student players, because it is a convenient size and easier to manipulate. The tenor is capable of enormous variety of tone and is the predominant solo saxophone. The baritone, with its considerable bulk and deep voice, is capable of great agility in the right hands.

soprano saxophone See saxophone

spirituals Traditional African-American religious songs.

stride piano Piano style in which the left hand marks the beat by vigorously "striding" forward. Fats Waller was its most famous exponent.

tenor saxophone See saxophone

timbales In Latin music, metal-shelled drums mounted in pairs and played with sticks.

tone The quality of a sound, for example, "harsh tone," "warm tone." Can sometimes refer to the pitch of a note, for example, "one tone higher."

vibraphone Tuned percussion instrument with metal bar chimes mounted above resonating tubes. Fans, driven by an electric motor and set between the bars and the tubes, cause the sound to oscillate, or vibrate.

TRUMPET & TROMBONE

The instrument most emblematic of jazz in its early decades was the trumpet. It was usually the loudest instrument, calling the shots as to what was played and how it was structured. Second-hand instruments from military bands, unemployed after the American Civil War, enabled the former slave population to adapt spirituals and hymns—and indeed marching music—in a celebration of freedom, tempered with the realities of life. New Orleans native Louis Armstrong typified this contrast within his playing (despite beginning on the quieter cornet, which has the same pitch as the trumpet), while his Chicago bandleader King Oliver's more subdued tone nevertheless exerted musical authority over his players. Equally suitable for both these roles was the trombone, capable of rousing backings to the lead role of the trumpet. The trombone's rhythmic blasts, and the slurs made by manipulating its slide, didn't preclude more virtuosic use in the 1920s by players such as Jack Teagarden, while in subsequent decades trombonists even tried to emulate the fluidity of saxophones. That was also true of later trumpet stylesetters, such as Dizzy Gillespie, while Miles Davis adopted a number of different approaches. He not only influenced the "cool" style of Chet Baker, but during the 1950s, he also popularized the flügelhorn as a mellow substitute for the trumpet.

3-SECOND RIFF
The trumpet's call to arms made it a natural lead instrument, but it has also proved capable of variety and subtlety.

3-MINUTE IMPROVISATION
Unlike other instruments, the tone of trumpets and trombones can be manipulated by the use of mutes, the earliest of which were the humble sinkplunger, the beer glass, human headgear, or even the human hand. Commercial versions of these implements were then manufactured, and the different sounds were well employed by the likes of King Oliver and Miles Davis, Ellington sidemen Bubber Miley, Cootie Williams, and his trombonist Joe Nanton.

RELATED TOPICS
See also
HOW THE PARTS FUNCTION
page 16

SAXOPHONE
page 56

LOUIS ARMSTRONG
page 64

MILES DAVIS
page 100

3-SECOND BIOGRAPHIES
JOE "KING" OLIVER
1885–1938
Cornet player and bandleader

JACK TEAGARDEN
1905–64
Trombonist, singer, and bandleader

JOHN "DIZZY" GILLESPIE
1917–93
Trumpeter and bandleader

EXPERT
Brian Priestley

Trumpets and trombones are key lead instruments, but their versatility means they can also be used with a more subtle effect.

SAXOPHONE

3-SECOND RIFF

The versatility of the saxophone makes it either strident or seductive and all the stages in between—it is the jazz symbol par excellence.

3-MINUTE IMPROVISATION

The saxophone is capable of a wide emotional range, partly because the combination of breath control and fingering is easier to manipulate than on brass instruments, such as the trumpet or trombone (confusingly, in pop and rock, saxophones are also termed as "brass"). It has also come to validate lengthy improvisation and experimentation—as Coleman Hawkins is alleged to have said, "If you don't make some mistakes, you're not really *trying*."

The visual representation of jazz these days is a saxophone. The instrument has, since the 1920s, been put to more expressive use in jazz than in other forms of music. Invented to simplify the note production of clarinets, and to combine that with the power of a brass instrument, the saxophone first found a place in military bands and then in circus orchestras. One early jazz player, Coleman Hawkins, turned the tenor sax into a viable vehicle for improvisation, inspired by the mobility of the clarinet and the trumpet playing of Louis Armstrong. Hawkins inspired players of the alto and baritone members of the sax family, such as Johnny Hodges and Harry Carney. The great variety of saxophone tone-quality—especially on the tenor—is illustrated by Lester Young, whose style is softspoken and oblique compared with the forthright preaching of Hawkins. The next great innovator, Charlie Parker, drew from aspects of both Young and Hawkins, while focusing on the alto and making it more powerful and cutting than was previously thought possible. Similarly, John Coltrane set a new standard with his penetrating tone on the tenor; he also reintroduced the almost forgotten soprano sax as a vehicle for extended improvisation, making it sound like a Middle Eastern or Indian instrument and opening the road towards "world music."

RELATED TOPICS

See also
TRUMPET & TROMBONE
page 54

CLARINET & FLUTE
page 58

CITIZENS OF THE WORLD
page 136

3-SECOND BIOGRAPHIES

JOHNNY HODGES
1906–70
Alto and soprano saxophonist

LESTER YOUNG
1909–59
Tenor saxophonist and clarinet player

JOHN COLTRANE
1926–67
Tenor and soprano saxophonist and bandleader

EXPERT

Brian Priestley

The saxophone lends itself well to improvisation and so has become vital to modern jazz.

CLARINET & FLUTE

3-SECOND RIFF
Popular in jazz from its early days, the clarinet was largely neglected after the mid-twentieth century, when orchestral woodwinds, such as the flute, came to prominence.

3-MINUTE IMPROVISATION
An interesting example of changing fashions in jazz, the clarinet's huge popularity during the 1930s–40s swing era may have contributed to its disfavor after the stylistic revolution of bebop. Similarly, the aural association of the flute with "cool jazz" condemned it for use in other styles, except that Yusef Lateef and Roland Kirk made it sound more muscular by humming and growling notes at the same time as playing them.

The clarinet, by virtue of its long history in military bands, was part of jazz much earlier than the saxophone, and, during the 1930s and 1940s, it became widely popular with the youth audience, especially in the hands of such players as Benny Goodman. That was also the heyday of the big bands, which habitually fielded a "reed section" of four or five saxophones, and, within such a section, one or more of the players would also be able to play on the clarinet and bass clarinet. The latter was rarely a solo instrument, but when it was, in the (very different) hands of Harry Carney or Eric Dolphy, it emulated the expressive tones of a sax. The regular clarinet, on the other hand, sounded relatively cold and quiet compared with the more heated jazz of the 1950s onward. Saxophone players now looking for a woodwind instrument, on which they could "double" their contribution, tended to adopt the flute, which, with the advent of amplification, could create adventurous improvisations in the manner of Rahsaan Roland Kirk. He was also renowned for hybrid saxophones called the manzello and strich, while remaining capable on standard instruments and sometimes playing two or three simultaneously. Some other prominent sax players have attempted the bassoon (Illinois Jacquet) and the oboe (Yusef Lateef), but these have never caught on.

RELATED TOPICS
See also
SWING
page 36

SAXOPHONE
page 56

3-SECOND BIOGRAPHIES
BENNY GOODMAN
1909–86
Clarinetist and bandleader

ERIC DOLPHY
1928–64
Alto saxophonist, clarinetist, bass clarinetist, and flutist

RAHSAAN ROLAND KIRK
1935–77
Tenor saxophonist and flutist

EXPERT
Brian Priestley

Benny Goodman helped to popularize the clarinet during the swing era, but it has fallen out of favor since then.

PIANO & KEYBOARDS

3-SECOND RIFF
Traditionally a solo instrument, the piano joined the jazz rhythm section but became a prominent lead voice, too, continuing both roles when electrified and synthesized.

3-MINUTE IMPROVISATION
In bygone days, when all music venues possessed an upright piano, many were in poor condition, so the arrival of electric keyboards in the 1950s was a boon to many touring musicians. The distinctive sound of the Fender Rhodes piano was mirrored by that of the 1935 Hammond organ, which had an instant response similar to that of the piano, making it possible to play rhythmically (unlike the pipe-organs found in movie theaters).

The role of the piano seems anomalous compared with the brass and reed instruments, being unsuitable for marching bands and usually played solo. The wide success of ragtime piano at the turn of the twentieth century popularized African-American rhythms with a strong admixture of European formats and harmonies. This proved the bridge to its acceptance in jazz, when players such as Earl Hines (versed in ragtime, or its virtuoso variant, "Harlem stride piano") began improvising solos and contributing to the impetus of rhythm sections—so the piano can be both a front-line and a back-line instrument within a single piece. Improved amplification liberated the piano to become the lead instrument of trios and quartets, or to be an orchestra in itself. Thelonious Monk, once criticized for not displaying a conventional fluency, gradually convinced listeners that his minimal chords and percussive attack were valid. On the other hand, Bill Evans's classical sound and impressionist harmonies seemed lacking in energy, yet many young pianists were captivated. This generation included Herbie Hancock and Chick Corea, who alternated playing acoustic piano with electric keyboards and synthesizers. In the same way, earlier players such as Jimmy Smith, took the electric organ and gave it a home in jazz and a distinctive sound.

RELATED TOPIC
See also
PIANO TRIO
page 148

3-SECOND BIOGRAPHIES
THELONIOUS MONK
1917–82
Pianist, composer, and bandleader

JIMMY SMITH
1925–2005
Electric organist and bandleader

BILL EVANS
1929–80
Pianist and bandleader

EXPERT
Brian Priestley

The piano can be part of both the front and back line. Thelonious Monk's unconventional playing eventually won over audiences.

BASS: DOUBLE BASS & BASS GUITAR

3-SECOND RIFF
The bass role has been fundamental—although initially unspectacular, it has changed thanks to later players of acoustic and electric instruments.

3-MINUTE IMPROVISATION
Hard for listeners to notice in the early days, the bass was also difficult for players themselves to hear accurately. After Duke Ellington featured Jimmie Blanton standing alongside the horns (even when just accompanying), his prominence led to the invention of a bass guitar, audible even in the loudest surroundings. Unfortunately, the amplification of double basses took a while to perfect, and some players (and sound engineers) made it far too prominent.

If you're initially attracted by the most exciting sounds in jazz, such as trumpets, saxophones, or percussion, you may not notice the bass instruments at all. But, just as ragtime piano became more streamlined for integration in a band, the fundamentals of harmony and marking the beat became a task for the bass. In early jazz, this was sometimes a brass instrument such as the tuba, and some early players were capable on both brass and string basses. But the latter proved most useful because, when plucked by someone like Jimmie Blanton, it provided a rhythmic noise that blended better with drums. Blanton also contributed a melodic approach to his function, and this inspired future exponents such as Charles Mingus, who made the bass a solo instrument. When first bass guitars and then, in the 1960s, specially designed electric basses appeared, a whole new sound was added to the jazz repertoire. Capable of filling the traditional role of the rhythm-section member, in the hands of Jaco Pastorius the bass was now able to take the lead, with haunting melodies played either alone or in unison with brass or reed players. Finally, it's worth mentioning that many bassists started on smaller string instruments, and there is a strong tradition of jazz violin playing, from Joe Venuti to Regina Carter.

RELATED TOPICS
See also
HOW THE PARTS FUNCTION
page 16

GUITAR: ACOUSTIC & ELECTRIC
page 68

3-SECOND BIOGRAPHIES
JIMMIE BLANTON
1918–42
Double bassist

CHARLES MINGUS
1922–79
Double bassist, composer, and bandleader

JACO PASTORIUS
1951–87
Electric bassist and bandleader

EXPERT
Brian Priestley

Initially used to mark the beat, advances in amplification mean the bass can also now be used as a lead instrument.

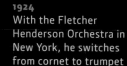

1901
Born in New Orleans

1922
Invited to Chicago to play second cornet in King Oliver's Creole Jazz Band

1924
With the Fletcher Henderson Orchestra in New York, he switches from cornet to trumpet

1925
Records as a leader for the Okeh label, producing a series of all-time jazz masterpieces

1926
His scat vocal style appears on record for the first time on "Heebie Jeebies"

1935–40
Tours and records with the Luis Russell Orchestra

1936
Appears in the movie *Pennies from Heaven*

1947
Forms the All Stars, a sextet that toured extensively for more than two decades and included, at various times, trombonists Trummy Young and Jack Teagarden, clarinetist Barney Bigard, and pianist Earl Hines

1964
"Hello Dolly" is released, soon knocking the Beatles' "Can't Buy Me Love" off the No. 1 spot in the United States

1968
"What a Wonderful World" is a No. 1 hit in the UK, where it becomes the best-selling single of the year

1971
Louis Armstrong dies of a heart attack at his home in Corona, Queens, New York, at the age of 69

LOUIS ARMSTRONG

Although not the first jazz musician, Louis Armstrong was the first truly great jazz musician and a wonderful ambassador for this new form of music. A superb trumpet player, instantly recognizable for his strong, clear sound and fine phrasing, he defined the art of the solo in jazz, bringing drama, sensitivity, and expression to his improvisations.

As befits a man who achieved legendary status early in his career and acquired two nicknames—Satchmo and Pops—some uncertainty traditionally surrounded Louis Armstrong's birth date. While he was adamant that it was July 4, 1900, (his mother called him the "firecracker boy"), birth records discovered in the 1980s confirmed that it was August 4, 1901. The young Louis grew up in a poor family in the Storyville area of New Orleans—notorious for its legalized brothels—and had a childhood of hard physical work. He joined a quartet of boys who sang in the streets for money, and would sneak into dance halls to listen to the bands and to the great Joe "King" Oliver playing jazz on cornet, a type of trumpet. Various misdemeanors, including the discharge of his stepfather's pistol during a New Year's Eve celebration, resulted in several periods spent in the New Orleans Home for Colored Waifs. There he received formal musical instruction and soon, with King Oliver as his mentor, he was playing in the clubs, parades, funerals, and on the riverboats of his native city.

In 1925, having honed his personal style with King Oliver's Creole Jazz Band and the Fletcher Henderson Orchestra, he began to record for the Okeh label. His Hot Five and Hot Seven recordings of "Cornet Chop Suey," "Potato Head Blues," and "West End Blues" (with its spectacular solo trumpet introduction) were enormously influential and remain jazz classics today. Armstrong's effervescent personality and good-natured humor found a parallel outlet through his improvised "scat singing" style. "Ain't Misbehavin," "Lazy River," and "Stardust" featured his innovative vocal interpretations alongside his superb trumpet playing, winning him a wide audience that transcended the racial boundaries of the time. His vocal style influenced not only Ella Fitzgerald, Billie Holiday, and almost every subsequent jazz singer, but also popular vocalists such as Bing Crosby and Frank Sinatra. Late in his career, he enjoyed a second burst of success with his hit records "Hello Dolly" and "What a Wonderful World." He died of a heart attack in 1971.

Charles Alexander

DRUMS & PERCUSSION

3-SECOND RIFF

The drummer, quietly competent or flamboyantly exciting, is crucial to jazz success. Incorporating Latin and African rhythms has brought in extra players and instruments.

3-MINUTE IMPROVISATION

In early, comparatively primitive situations, percussion was achieved by using thimbles on a washboard—compare this with the elaborate setups of post-rock players, with multiple tom-toms and a variety of cymbals. Any individual components can produce effects from the grandiose to the subtle, and it's worth noting that many jazz drummers borrowed their rhythmic ideas from tap-dancing, some performers, such as Jo Jones or Buddy Rich, being adept at both.

A drum kit being played expertly is one of the most compelling sights in jazz and, while a rock drummer may concentrate on power and propulsion, a jazz drummer can often fulfill the same role with considerably more subtlety. The basic kit of snare drum, bass drum, and cymbals, played by separate individuals in marching bands, was assembled for a single sitting musician in the early twentieth century. Its role in propelling other band members, and being a center of attention for listeners, was established by stars, such as Gene Krupa and Buddy Rich, while the complex pulses of mid-century jazz were personified by Art Blakey. He also played a part in incorporating the South American rhythms employed by Afro-Latin bands; since these have become more common, it's not unusual to see instruments such as congas, maracas, or timbales, added to the rhythm section. This often requires an additional player or two, and in bands that do only occasional Latin numbers, it can be trumpeters or saxophone players who are expected to provide the extra percussion sounds. The vibraphone (an electrified marimba, descended from African instruments) was adopted from the 1920s onward by performers who usually started out as drummers, such as the pioneer Lionel Hampton and the Latin-jazz bandleader Tito Puente.

RELATED TOPIC

See also
HOW THE PARTS FUNCTION
page 16

3-SECOND BIOGRAPHIES

LIONEL HAMPTON
1908–2002
Vibraphonist, drummer, and bandleader

GENE KRUPA
1909–73
Drummer and bandleader

ART BLAKEY
1919–90
Drummer and bandleader

EXPERT
Brian Priestley

The jazz drummer can be a focus for the audience's attention. Gene Krupa (center) brought energy to the stage. Lionel Hampton (top left) helped introduce the vibraphone to jazz.

GUITAR: ACOUSTIC & ELECTRIC

3-SECOND RIFF

Like the bass in jazz, guitar was at first a rhythm instrument, which, since amplification, has blossomed into an improvising vehicle of great variety and excitement.

3-MINUTE IMPROVISATION

The strumming of an acoustic guitar in early jazz was closely akin to its use in folk music. The liberation of its melodic potential arose from jazz and passed into pop and rock. Significantly, the arrival of effects pedals allowed what was fingered as a single-note line to be, for instance, artificially harmonized or distorted. In jazz terms, this allowed a variation of tonecolors typical of saxophones or even an emulation of brass mutes.

The guitar is so prominent in jazz that it comes as a shock to learn it only established itself in the 1940s. The acoustic instrument was previously used, in the same manner as the banjo, as a contributor to the rhythm section along with bass and drums, often playing just backing chords. Those few earlier musicians who began to develop it as a solo improvising instrument, such as Eddie Lang and the "Gypsy jazz" virtuoso Django Reinhardt, often had problems being heard alongside brass or percussion. The advent of amplification meant the pioneering work of Charlie Christian could create single-note, sax-type lines on an equal footing with actual saxophones. Many followers have extended Christian's style, notably Wes Montgomery who dispensed with the banjo-type plectrum (or "pick") and used his thumb to obtain a softer but no less rhythmic sound. As one of the most prominent overlaps with rock music, the guitar in jazz often draws on its heritage as a traditional blues instrument, while other variations in the way the guitar is heard have been adapted directly from rock or world music. For instance, the virtuosic work of John McLaughlin frequently uses a double-necked instrument—one neck having the conventional six strings, the other with the folky sound of a twelve-string guitar.

RELATED TOPICS

See also
HOW THE PARTS FUNCTION
page 16

JAZZ ROCK & FUSION
page 46

BASS: DOUBLE BASS
& BASS GUITAR
page 62

ELECTRIC GUITAR BLUES
page 128

3-SECOND BIOGRAPHIES
DJANGO REINHARDT
1910–53
Guitarist and bandleader

WES MONTGOMERY
1923–68
Guitarist and bandleader

JOHN MCLAUGHLIN
1942–
Guitarist and bandleader

EXPERT
Brian Priestley

Since amplification, the guitar has taken a more prominent role in jazz.

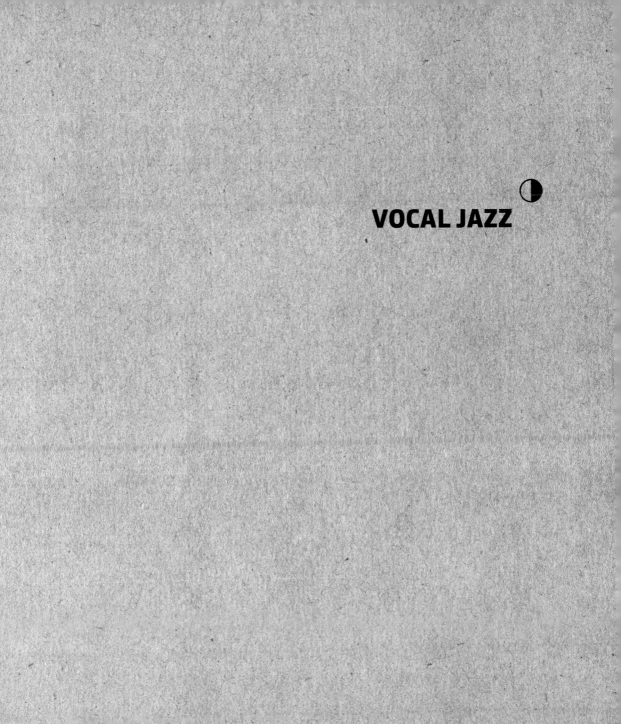

VOCAL JAZZ

VOCAL JAZZ
GLOSSARY

big band Normally a band of around sixteen players, arranged in sections—trumpets, trombones, saxophones, rhythm. This format evolved in the late 1920s and early 1930s as the standard American dance orchestra, reaching its apotheosis in the swing era of the late 1930s. Big bands for dancing declined in popularity after World War II, but a few of those with a jazz reputation survived or soon reformed—notably those of Count Basie, Duke Ellington, and Woody Herman. They played mainly to concert audiences and were joined by others, such as Stan Kenton's orchestra and the Gerry Mulligan Concert Band. In more recent times, the standard big-band formula has grown somewhat stiff and predictable, relying on complex arrangements and virtuosic ensemble playing.

close harmony In vocal music, a blend of voices with the individual parts as close together as possible.

contralto The lower of the two ranges of the female voice.

Dixieland jazz An early style of jazz first recorded in 1917 by the Original Dixieland Jazz Band and still practiced today, mainly by white musicians.

Great Depression A severe economic slump that began with the collapse of the New York stock market in October 1929 (the "Wall Street Crash") and spread from the United States to the rest of the industrialized world, causing mass poverty and unemployment. The effects lasted until the outbreak of war in Europe in 1939.

hipster A phenomenon of the 1950s and early 1960s. One who presented himself as being "hip"—familiar with the most advanced ideas and trends, especially in music. A hipster was in advance of fashion and scornful of those with conventional tastes ("squares").

Hit Parade List of the most popular songs and records in the United States, issued by music publishers, record companies, and broadcasters.

jive talk Slang or argot employed in the swing era by musicians and their adherents.

melisma Ornate melodic decoration of a vocal line, widely used in gospel and soul music.

minstrel Now widely regarded as having been demeaning to African-American people, minstrel shows were variety performances in which performers appeared in "blackface" makeup. The material commonly consisted of sentimental songs, eccentric dancing, and comedy routines representing black people as idle and stupid. Both black and white minstrel troupes were popular in parts of the United States between the end of the American Civil War and the outbreak of World War II.

octave The span of eight degrees in the diatonic scale; the distance from a given note to the next note of the same name above or below. A handy example is the first two notes of the song "Over The Rainbow": the two syllables of the word "somewhere" are an octave apart.

scatting Singing wordless syllables in imitation of an instrumental solo.

soprano The higher of the two ranges of the female voice.

swing Two meanings: 1) A style of jazz that emerged in the 1930s and is widely supposed to have been supplanted by bebop. 2) A rhythmic phenomenon, unique to jazz, arising from the tension between a steady, metric pulse and a rhythmically free melodic line. Requests for a definition of swing are often met with the variously attributed riposte, "If you have to ask what it is, you ain't got it!"

zoot suit A male fashion of the postwar 1940s, characterized by a loose-fitting draped jacket with padded shoulders, worn with tapered pants.

DIVAS

3-SECOND RIFF
A jazz singer is hard to define, because there is no clear dividing line between, say, blues, jazz, and popular singing.

3-MINUTE IMPROVISATION
Unlike classical singers, most jazz vocalists perform in their everyday voices. They can't easily be labeled as soprano, contralto, etc., and their individual vocal equipment varies wildly. Billie had a tiny range of little more than an octave, and a somewhat thin voice. Ella's warm, velvety tones could reach well up into the soprano range. The pitch of Sarah's voice dropped with age. Toward the end, she was touching on the baritone register.

Each of the three acknowledged "divas" of jazz represents one of the fundamental qualities of the genre. Billie Holiday, in her early career, sang with perfect simplicity, her small, bright voice elegantly reshaping every song and setting it gently swinging. Later, as drugs, alcohol, and abusive men darkened her life, her singing darkened too, telling gritty tales of loss and betrayal. She was a pure artist, never seeking to ingratiate herself with an audience, telling it straight and singing the only way she knew how. Ella Fitzgerald had the smoothest, most flexible voice imaginable and could switch effortlessly from singing a romantic ballad with a string orchestra to scatting wildly with a band of jazz musicians. Even at her most animated, there was an unruffled and undisturbed calm about Ella's singing that brought her lasting popularity far beyond the jazz world. The third diva is Sarah Vaughan. She was a child of bebop, where her remarkable vocal range and superb ear captivated musicians and audiences alike. Throughout her career, her sheer delight in the physical act of singing was an important part of her charm and could leave audiences gasping. The three qualities? A personal sound (Ella), appropriate technique (Sarah), and, above all, truth (Billie).

RELATED TOPICS
See also
BEBOP TO HARD BOP
page 40

GREAT AMERICAN
SONGBOOK: THE WOMEN
page 78

ELLA FITZGERALD
page 82

SCAT & VOCALESE
page 86

3-SECOND BIOGRAPHIES
BILLIE HOLIDAY
1915–59
Singer and occasional lyricist

ELLA FITZGERALD
1917–96
Singer

SARAH VAUGHAN
1924–90
Singer and occasional pianist

EXPERT
Dave Gelly

Each of the three great divas brought her own unique style to jazz performance, both when recording and singing live.

GREAT AMERICAN SONGBOOK: THE MEN

3-SECOND RIFF

Although there is no actual Great American Songbook, the popular songs that make up its contents have formed the basis for many performers' repertoires.

3-MINUTE IMPROVISATION

Standard songs often have their origins in Broadway musicals or Hollywood movies; others were first heard on the radio, sung either live or on record. But it was the song itself, not any particular version, that survived. The original Hit Parade was based not on record sales but on sales of sheet music. This encouraged singers and instrumentalists to create their own interpretations, while also providing them with a ready source of material.

Jazz grew up as part of American popular culture. The first jazz singers were popular singers, singing popular songs of the day. By the middle of the twentieth century, the best of these songs—by composers such as Irving Berlin, George Gershwin, and Cole Porter—had become the basis of a vast standard repertoire, often called the Great American Songbook. Over the years, singers of very different styles built their own repertoires from this source. Bing Crosby began his career as one of The Rhythm Boys, a vocal trio, with Paul Whiteman's band, and retained the loose, easy Dixieland approach until the end of his life. Frank Sinatra took Crosby as his first model before joining The Harry James Orchestra in 1939 and developing his own style, based on swing. Nat King Cole, a brilliant jazz pianist before he ever sang a note, came to be accepted as the leading exponent of romantic ballads in his generation. His appeal owed much to the elegance and rhythmic ease of his phrasing, qualities rooted in his jazz background. Mel Tormé brought some of the complexity and brilliance of bebop to his treatment of material drawn from that same great storehouse of songs.

RELATED TOPICS

See also
SWING
page 36

BEBOP TO HARD BOP
page 40

GREAT AMERICAN SONGBOOK: THE WOMEN
page 78

3-SECOND BIOGRAPHIES

BING CROSBY
1903–77
Singer, movie star, and occasional songwriter

FRANK SINATRA
1915–98
Singer and movie star

NAT KING COLE
1919–65
Singer, pianist, and movie star

MEL TORMÉ
1925–99
Singer, arranger, pianist, drummer, and author

EXPERT
Dave Gelly

Jazz singers such as Frank Sinatra, Nat King Cole, and Frankie Lane had mass appeal.

GREAT AMERICAN SONGBOOK: THE WOMEN

Things are changing now, but apart from some pianists, there have been few women instrumentalists in jazz. On the other hand, women dominate the history of jazz singing. Adelaide Hall shocked listeners in 1927 with her throaty, feline growl. Mildred Bailey, Maxine Sullivan, and Lena Horne were stars of the swing era who spent their entire careers working alongside the best jazz musicians of the day. In the 1950s, Julie London, singing in little more than a whisper, recorded exquisite miniatures with minimal accompaniment. Anita O'Day showed a new generation the way into bebop. And Peggy Lee, who was once told by Louis Armstrong that she was "born to swing," not only enjoyed a long and glorious career but also wrote songs with both Duke Ellington and Quincy Jones. And they all depended on the Great American Songbook—in Peggy's case adding a few of her own to it. The variety of styles and voices among these jazz singers is endless. Some didn't even call themselves "jazz singers"—Julie London, for instance described herself as a "song stylist." There's no handy definition. A jazz singer is one who is accepted by jazz musicians and listeners as one of their own.

RELATED TOPIC

See also
GREAT AMERICAN SONGBOOK: THE MEN
page 76

3-SECOND BIOGRAPHIES

ADELAIDE HALL
1901–93
Singer and musical-comedy actress

MILDRED BAILEY
1907–51
Singer

MAXINE SULLIVAN
1911–87
Singer and musical-comedy actress

LENA HORNE
1917–2010
Singer and movie star

ANITA O'DAY
1919–2006
Singer

EXPERT
Dave Gelly

Jazz has a rich history of female singers, such as the stars of swing Mildred Bailey, Lena Horne, and Maxine Sullivan.

JAZZ ENTERTAINERS

The jazz subculture of the 1930s
and 1940s had its own dress code (the zoot
suit), lingo (jive talk), and cult leader, Cab
Calloway, the world's first black "superdude."
He dressed crazy, talked crazy, sang crazy, and
led one of the best swing bands in the land.
After that, the old minstrel stereotype of the
black entertainer was dead. Along with Cab
came Fats Waller, a virtuoso pianist and a
songwriter of near-genius, who simply couldn't
keep his sense of humor in check, with
gloriously chaotic results. When World War II
began, Louis Jordan, the GI's favorite, reached
the height of his fame. Central to his image were
tales of overindulgence, misbehavior, and
explaining the events of the night before to the
judge on the morning after. With bebop, Slim
Gaillard appeared, apparently from outer space.
He could play the piano with his knuckles, spoke
four languages, and invented another one, all
his own, to amuse his public of cool cats and
hipsters. In the early 1950s, a crop of down-to-
earth female singer-pianists caught the public's
attention. Many of their songs were sternly
addressed to reluctant or unsatisfactory men.
The jovial Nellie Lutcher made a particularly big
splash. After that, the tradition of popular jazz
entertainers almost came to an end, although
a few occasionally popped up later—Great
Britain's George Melly, for instance.

3-SECOND BIOGRAPHIES
FATS WALLER
1904–43
Pianist, organist, singer,
and composer

CAB CALLOWAY
1907–94
Singer, bandleader,
and showman

LOUIS JORDAN
1908–75
Saxophonist, singer,
and bandleader

SLIM GAILLARD
1916–91
Pianist, guitarist, singer,
songwriter, and actor

EXPERT
Dave Gelly

*During hard times, the
public turned to artists,
such as Cab Calloway
and Louis Jordan, for
entertainment.*

1917
Born in Newport News,
Virginia

1935
Joins the Chick Webb
Orchestra at the Savoy
Ballroom, Harlem, New
York

1943
Signs with Decca Records
as a solo artist

1949
Her first appearance with
Jazz at the Philharmonic

1956
Records *The Cole Porter
Songbook* album, the
first of a classic series

1987
Receives the National
Medal for the Arts from
President Reagan

1989
Retires because of ill
health

1996
Dies in Beverly Hills,
California

ELLA FITZGERALD

There is no purer, more limpid sound in American music than Ella Fitzgerald's voice singing "Ev'ry Time We Say Goodbye." By contrast, nothing expresses better the sheer joie de vivre of jazz at its most energetic than her scat-bebop version of "How High The Moon." She was a singer of astonishing variety, and left to posterity one of the largest bodies of recorded work in history.

Ella was born in Newport News, Virginia, on April 25, 1917. She had an unfortunate childhood, and by her mid-teens was living as a vagrant on the streets of Harlem. In 1934, despite her bedraggled appearance, she won the amateur talent contest that launched her career. The following year she joined Chick Webb's band at the Savoy Ballroom and made her recording debut. Her first hit record, "A-Tisket, A-Tasket," was made with Webb in 1938.

Chick Webb died in 1939, and after a period in which she acted as the band's nominal leader, Ella began her solo career. Signed to Decca records, she soon became one of the leading popular singers of the day. On the strength of a hit record, "My Happiness," she made her first overseas appearance at the London Palladium in 1948.

The following year she joined the all-star package show, Jazz At The Philharmonic, organized by the impresario Norman Granz, who was to promote and guide her career until the end. In 1955, when her Decca contract expired, she signed with Granz's label, Verve. Hitherto, Ella's remarkable stylistic range had been employed in a somewhat haphazard manner. Ballads, swing tunes, duet pieces—they had not been released according to any coherent plan. Granz now set about making the most of a talent that he knew would appeal to an even more diverse public.

Thus, in 1956, Ella recorded *The Cole Porter Songbook*, the first in a long series of lavishly produced albums devoted to the classic American song and its leading creators. She was soon established not only as one of the greatest of all jazz singers but as a concert artist, too. The albums for Verve and its successor, Pablo, represent the work of Ella Fitzgerald's maturity in all its diversity and richness.

From the very beginning until well into her sixties, Ella's voice kept its bloom of youthful innocence, and her diction, as Cole Porter once observed, was faultless. She retired in 1989 and died in 1996.

Dave Gelly

VOCAL GROUPS

3-SECOND RIFF
The sound of a typical vocal group is so distinctive that it can instantly conjure up the whole era of the late 1930s and 1940s.

3-MINUTE IMPROVISATION
There is a particular sound to most vocal groups, quite unlike that of a traditional choir. It is called "close harmony." The vocal lines are literally closer together, and they move in formation, like a flock of birds. Written down, the parts would look much like the score for a saxophone section. Indeed, some groups, The Pied Pipers, for instance, could sound remarkably like four saxophones—alto, two tenors, and baritone.

Although often overlooked,

vocal groups—three or more voices together in harmony—play an important part in the history of jazz singing. The Boswell Sisters caused a sensation in 1931, with their version of Louis Armstrong's "Heebie Jeebies." They showed how, using close harmony and pinpoint phrasing, any tune could be made to swing. They had many imitators, among them the hugely popular Andrews Sisters. Big bands in the swing era often included a vocal group as well as solo singers. These were generally composed of mixed men's and women's voices, examples being The Pied Pipers (who performed with Tommy Dorsey's band) and The Modernaires (with Glenn Miller). Intricate arrangements and virtuoso performances were the hallmarks of two male quartets, The Four Freshmen and The Hi-Lo's, who won awards for their albums with jazz instrumentalists in the 1950s. In the 1960s, it seemed that the vocal-group tradition in jazz had died out in the face of competition from rock music. There were, however, The Swingle Singers, who scored a surprise success with swinging, wordless versions of Baroque classics. The Manhattan Transfer, an extraordinary quartet of two women and two men, arrived in the 1970s. They were at home in every popular idiom of the twentieth century, especially swing and R&B.

RELATED TOPICS
See also
SWING
page 36

GREAT AMERICAN SONGBOOK: THE MEN
page 76

GREAT AMERICAN SONGBOOK: THE WOMEN
page 78

3-SECOND BIOGRAPHIES
CONNIE BOSWELL
1907–76
Eldest member and lead singer of The Boswell Sisters

JO STAFFORD
1917–2008
Member of The Pied Pipers and later a popular solo artist

TIM HAUSER
1941–2014
Singer; founder and leader of The Manhattan Transfer

EXPERT
Dave Gelly

Vocal groups such as The Modernaires, blended male and female voices to create close harmonies.

SCAT & VOCALESE

These two types of singing are almost exclusively confined to jazz. Scat is vocal improvisation using nonsense syllables in place of words. A famous early example is Louis Armstrong's "Heebie Jeebies" (1926). In this, his scat improvisation precisely matches his trumpet style. Cab Calloway popularized scat with "The Scat Song" in 1932. Some vocal groups, such as The Mills Brothers, imitated the sound of instruments when scatting. Ella Fitzgerald was so admired for her virtuosity with scat, including instrumental imitation, that she influenced singers of several generations. Scat singing helped popularize bebop—indeed, the term itself is a fragment of scat. Several of Dizzy Gillespie's numbers had scat titles, such as "Oop Bop Sh'Bam" and "Ool Ya Koo." Wordless singing continues in various jazz styles to this day. Vocalese is the difficult art of inventing a coherent text to fit a recorded jazz solo. Among the earliest vocalese artists were King Pleasure and Eddie Jefferson, but the piece that captured most attention was "Twisted," set to a Wardell Gray saxophone solo by Annie Ross, who first recorded it in 1952. The undoubted master of the genre, however, is Jon Hendricks. His work, notably for the groups Lambert, Hendricks & Ross and The Manhattan Transfer, reveals a verbal facility little short of genius.

3-SECOND RIFF
Scat brings the full flexibility of the human voice to jazz improvisation. Vocalese calls for verbal ingenuity and musical skill of a high order.

3-MINUTE IMPROVISATION
With Louis Armstrong, especially, scat is a hovering presence in all his singing. He inserts syllables, chuckles, and grunts to complete or turn a phrase. These are always harmonically and melodically apt, never random. With vocalese, it is not enough simply for the words to fit the music; they must either tell an amusing story—like "Twisted"—or have some reference to the original soloist—like "Parker's Mood," by King Pleasure.

RELATED TOPICS
See also
BEBOP TO HARD BOP
page 40

LOUIS ARMSTRONG
page 64

JAZZ ENTERTAINERS
page 80

ELLA FITZGERALD
page 82

VOCAL GROUPS
page 84

3-SECOND BIOGRAPHIES
JON HENDRICKS
1921–2017
Singer and songwriter

ANNIE ROSS
1930–
Singer, actress, and occasional songwriter

EXPERT
Dave Gelly

Louis Armstrong and Ella Fitzgerald were masters of the scat style of improvisation.

CONTEMPORARIES

From the 1960s, the prominence of the Great American Songbook gradually faded in the face of developments in jazz and popular music. Probably the most powerful of these was soul music, especially the recordings of Ray Charles, whose late-1950s albums on Atlantic Records were immensely influential. It is rare nowadays to encounter a singer with jazz connections who does not employ, at least occasionally, the multinote expressive effect known as "melisma." This characteristic of soul and gospel music is completely absent from the swing style of Billie Holiday or Ella Fitzgerald, but appears often in the work of their late-twentieth-century successors, for instance, Diane Reeves and Dee Dee Bridgewater. In the same period, jazz ceased to be a purely American music. The European avant-garde included singers such as Urszula Dudziak, who mingled jazz rock with Polish folksong; the Norwegian Karin Krog, whose repertoire reached from standard songs to complete abstraction; and Norma Winstone, a leading figure in the British jazz scene from the 1970s onward. Some vocalists continued in the broad tradition of jazz singing, among them Gregory Porter and singer-pianist Diana Krall. And, as ever, there have been occasional artists, such as Bobby McFerrin, who fit into no category other than that of virtuoso.

RELATED TOPICS
See also
BOSSA NOVA TO FREEDOM
page 44

EUROPEAN JAZZ
page 48

3-SECOND RIFF
Jazz singing followed popular taste by picking up on soul music, while at the same time taking in new influences from Europe and elsewhere.

3-MINUTE IMPROVISATION
Because singing and language are closely interwoven, vocal jazz has been slow in adopting elements of world music. It is still normal for European singers to perform in English, basing their repertoire on classic American songs. Bossa Nova, in the early 1960s, was an exception, but even here Brazilian Portuguese was often replaced by lyrics in English. Whatever the reason, apart from scat and avant-garde abstraction, English remains overwhelmingly the language of jazz.

3-SECOND BIOGRAPHIES
KARIN KROG
1937–
Norwegian singer

NORMA WINSTONE
1941–
British singer and lyricist

DEE DEE BRIDGEWATER
1950–
American singer

EXPERT
Dave Gelly

Soul music has entered jazz through the vocal styles of singers, such as Ray Charles and Dee Dee Bridgewater.

STEREO ONE

CLASSIC JAZZ ALBUMS

CLASSIC JAZZ ALBUMS
GLOSSARY

acoustic Literally, to do with the sense of hearing. Main uses of this adjective in jazz are: 1) "unamplified," referring to instruments (such as acoustic guitar) or unamplified music generally; 2) referring to the effect of the physical surroundings where music is played on the listening experience (acoustic conditions). The noun "acoustics" is applied to this whole topic.

big band Normally a band of around sixteen players, arranged in sections—trumpets, trombones, saxophones, rhythm. This format evolved in the late 1920s and early 1930s as the standard American dance orchestra, reaching its apotheosis in the swing era of the late 1930s. Big bands for dancing declined in popularity after World War II, but a few of those with a jazz reputation survived or soon reformed—notably those of Count Basie, Duke Ellington, and Woody Herman. They now played mainly to concert audiences and were joined by others, such as Stan Kenton's orchestra and the Gerry Mulligan Concert Band. In more recent times, the standard big-band formula has grown somewhat stiff and predictable, relying on complex arrangements and virtuosic ensemble playing.

chord progression The series of harmonies ("chords") underlying a melody. More usually called "chord sequence."

cool jazz A restrained, undemonstrative style of jazz that emerged in the early 1950s, possibly in reaction to the vehemence of bebop. Leading early exponents included Stan Getz, Lee Konitz, and the young Miles Davis. The aesthetic of "cool" went beyond mere style to embrace an attitude of self-contained detachment toward the world at large. The exemplar for both style and attitude was the saxophonist Lester Young, said to have been the first to use the word "cool" as a term of approbation.

fusion music Any synthesis of jazz with rock, soul, funk, pop, etc.

mode scales Musical scales, other than the standard major and minor scales, used as a basis for improvisation.

nonet A band of nine players.

quintet A band of five players.

rhythm section Literally, the instruments and their players generating the "rhythm." Nowadays, it consists almost always of the bass and drums. In prebebop styles the guitar is generally also present and in preswing styles the banjo. The piano commonly plays a dual role, acting as part of the rhythm section when accompanying and as a solo instrument at other times.

section writing Written score for the brass, saxophone rhythm sections of a big band.

sextet A band of six players.

stride piano Piano style in which the left hand marks the beat by vigorously "striding" forward. Fats Waller was its most famous exponent.

studio musician A musician employed wholly or largely in radio or recording studios.

synthesizer An electronic instrument that generates and processes sound. Used mainly by players of keyboard instruments to extend their range of available sounds and effects. The composers Gil Evans and Quincy Jones both made extensive use of synthesizers in the 1970s and 1980s, as did Herbie Hancock and other keyboard artists.

territory bands Touring bands of the 1930s, which confined themselves to a certain area or "territory." They catered particularly to the scattered communities of the large southwestern states, such as Texas, Oklahoma, Missouri, and Kansas.

vibraphone Tuned percussion instrument with metal bar chimes mounted above resonating tubes. Fans, driven by an electric motor and set between the bars and the tubes, cause the sound to oscillate, or vibrate.

LOUIS ARMSTRONG
SATCH PLAYS FATS

3-SECOND RIFF

Fats Waller's charm and melodic genius permeates these entertaining songs and inspires some of Louis Armstrong's most relaxed, lyrical trumpet playing and singing.

3-MINUTE IMPROVISATION

For its first fifty years, most jazz musicians either played the compositions of bandleaders such as Fats Waller or Duke Ellington or improvised upon the melodies and chord progressions of the Great American Songbook —popular songs from musicals and movies. From the early 1950s, popular music became less attractive and interesting for jazz players to work with, and today most jazz musicians write some, if not all, of the music that they perform.

Louis Armstrong played with

Fats Waller for only a brief period in 1925, in Chicago, but the charismatic trumpeter so admired this extraordinary pianist and loved Fats's songs that thirty years later he recorded eleven of them as a tribute. Nine of these were released by Columbia on the 1955 LP *Satch Plays Fats*. The two remaining songs and nine alternative takes are included on a Sony CD reissue. After receiving piano lessons as a boy, Fats Waller learned to play the stride style of James P. Johnson. A gifted composer, Fats would turn out perfectly crafted songs in almost no time at all, invariably in partnership with lyricist Andy Razaf, and sing them with great wit and charm. This talent propelled him into the world of musical comedy and from there to international stardom. Armstrong, by now in the later years of his stellar career, clearly enjoyed sharing the pleasure of "(What Did I Do to Be So) Black and Blue," "Squeeze Me," "Ain't Misbehavin," and other fine Waller songs with clarinetist Barney Bigard and trombonist Trummy Young. His trumpet playing is technically superb with a wonderful full sound in all registers, and his phrases are all perfectly placed, often finishing with an expressive flourish of vibrato. His joyful vocal duet with Velma Middleton on "Honeysuckle Rose" makes the ideal opener for this delightful album.

RELATED TOPICS

See also
NEW ORLEANS
& CLASSIC JAZZ
page 34

TRUMPET & TROMBONE
page 54

LOUIS ARMSTRONG
page 64

3-SECOND BIOGRAPHIES
LOUIS ARMSTRONG
1901–71
First major jazz star; trumpet player, vocalist, and bandleader

FATS WALLER
1904–43
Jazz pianist, organist, songwriter, and bandleader

BARNEY BIGARD
1906–80
Jazz clarinetist with Duke Ellington and Louis Armstrong

EXPERT
Charles Alexander

Armstrong's 1955 album was a tribute to the great bandleader Fats Waller (far right).

BENNY GOODMAN
THE COMPLETE LEGENDARY 1938 CARNEGIE HALL CONCERT

3-SECOND RIFF
The acclaim for Benny Goodman's 1938 Carnegie Hall concert brought jazz into the concert hall and also highlighted the artistry of its African-American innovators.

3-MINUTE IMPROVISATION
The success of Benny Goodman's 1938 concert helped raise the profile of jazz from that of mere entertainment to an art form — one performed by dedicated musicians that deserved to be presented in concert halls and appreciated alongside classical music. While his single-minded determination was a major factor, it was no hindrance that he was also a virtuoso classical clarinetist who would record Mozart's "Clarinet Quintet" with the Budapest String Quartet three months later.

On January 16, 1938, clarinetist and bandleader Benny Goodman, the "King of Swing," performed at New York's Carnegie Hall. Goodman was already the most famous white jazz musician in the country, but this would be the first jazz concert ever held in this prestigious classical-music venue. It was therefore vital both for Goodman's career and the status of jazz that it was a success. But this was not the only boundary to be crossed; the other was race. The theme of the concert was "20 Years of Jazz," and to honour some of the musicians who had defined those first two decades Goodman augmented his regular big band with saxophonists Johnny Hodges and Harry Carney and trumpeter Cootie Williams from the Duke Ellington band and Count Basie with his tenor-sax star Lester Young, all African-Americans. Goodman also featured his regular quartet, which included two African-American musicians, pianist Teddy Wilson, and vibraphonist Lionel Hampton—a bold but controversial step. The concert opened with the swinging "Don't Be That Way" performed by Goodman's big band with both the first few bars of trumpet star Harry James's solo and a formidable drum break from Gene Krupa, inspiring spontaneous rounds of applause. Fortunately, the concert was recorded and broadcast two days later on the radio.

RELATED TOPICS
See also
SWING
page 36

SAXOPHONE
page 56

CLARINET & FLUTE
page 58

3-SECOND BIOGRAPHIES
JOHNNY HODGES
1906–70
Bandleader and alto saxophonist with Duke Ellington

LESTER YOUNG
1909–59
Tenor saxophonist with the Count Basie Orchestra

BENNY GOODMAN
1909–86
Clarinetist, composer, and bandleader

EXPERT
Charles Alexander

Benny Goodman's concert broke both musical and racial conventions.

COUNT BASIE
THE ATOMIC MR. BASIE

3-SECOND RIFF
Neal Hefti's exciting arrangements and a brilliant edition of the Basie band were the formula for this classic big-band album.

3-MINUTE IMPROVISATION
The 1950s were a fruitful period for the big band, as bandleaders such as Duke Ellington, Woody Herman, Dizzy Gillespie, and Stan Kenton, sought to broaden its palette with bebop sounds, Afro-Cuban rhythms, and contemporary classical-music devices. By the 1960s, financial difficulties had driven many big bands off the road, but the Basie band, with its great arrangements and blues and swing roots, continued to flourish many years after its leader's death in 1984.

Throughout the 1930s, "territory" bands traveled throughout the southern states, playing dance music in ballrooms. Many of these big bands featured great jazz players plus fine arrangers to shape the sound and style of the band. Formed in Kansas City, the Count Basie Orchestra hit New York in 1936 with a big-band style that swung hard and simply dripped with the blues. In the early 1950s, Basie assembled a new edition of the band. Shifting its emphasis from soloists to repertoire, he commissioned the best arrangers of the day to write for it. In 1957, the band recorded *The Atomic Mr. Basie* (originally titled $E=MC^2$) with eleven tunes, all composed and arranged by Neal Hefti. The opening track, "Kid from Red Bank," features the leader's piano and his trademark style—short phrases placed for utmost rhythmic effect. The power and sheer precision of the saxophone and brass sections shines through, whether on the relaxed "After Supper" or the breathtaking "Flight of the Foo Birds." Hefti created cameos for particular players—"Duet" for trumpeters Joe Newman and Thad Jones and the gentle "Li'l Darlin" for Wendell Culley's muted trumpet—but ultimately it is his strong melodies, exciting rhythms, and excellent section writing for this great band that make it such a significant big-band jazz album.

RELATED TOPICS
See also
ORCHESTRAL JAZZ
page 38

BIG BANDS & THE BLUES
page 122

3-SECOND BIOGRAPHIES
WILLIAM "COUNT" BASIE
1904–84
Jazz pianist, bandleader, and composer

EDDIE "LOCKJAW" DAVIS
1922–86
Saxophonist and bandleader

NEAL HEFTI
1922–2008
Trumpeter, composer, arranger, and songwriter

EXPERT
Charles Alexander

The Atomic Mr. Basie *is one of the most acclaimed big-band jazz albums.*

$=mc^2$

Born in Alton, Illinois

1945
Moves to New York, plays on Charlie Parker's first featured records

Leads short-lived nonet, later called the Birth Of The Cool

1955
Forms first quintet, featuring John Coltrane

1957
Records first big-band album *Miles Ahead*

Records *Kind Of Blue*, which eventually becomes the best-selling jazz album ever

1963
Another influential quintet, with Herbie Hancock and eventually Wayne Shorter

1969
Bitches Brew album cements the incorporation of rock music

1991
Dies in Santa Monica, California

MILES DAVIS

Like many illustrious performers, Miles Davis cultivated his charisma as a way of ensuring an audience. But, unlike earlier jazzmen such as Louis Armstrong and Duke Ellington, who worked at ingratiating themselves, Davis adopted an air of indifference to his listeners, especially white listeners. This attitude grabbed the audience's attention, and Davis actually promoted several white players, including pianist Bill Evans and guitarist John Scofield.

A similarity with Ellington is seen in Davis's ability to leave leeway to the players in his groups, while retaining a subtle control over the total outcome. This stemmed from his early realization that he was no virtuoso on the trumpet, easily overawed by players such as Charlie Parker and Dizzy Gillespie. At nineteen years old when he first recorded with Parker, Davis had already acquired a beguilingly reticent tone, a consistent asset even when he developed a tightly muted sound in the 1950s.

His playing achieved enormous influence, but his various band styles did so even more. The highly arranged nonet inaugurated in 1948 helped create a whole subgenre called "cool jazz," whose approach was expanded on the big band albums *Miles Ahead*, *Porgy And Bess*, and *Sketches Of Spain*. But the contemporaneous quintets and sextets, best known for *Kind Of Blue*, were equally influential because of the freedom allowed to the individual members.

All the above developments retain their devoted fans, to whom it came as a shock when the "second quintet" established in 1963, gradually started to include the electric bass, electric keyboard, and eventually electric guitar. The album that confirmed there was to be no turning back, *Bitches Brew*, was Davis's fastest-selling album at the time and gained a new younger audience, which continued to respect him as a figurehead. The decibel level meant the trumpeter himself had to be amplified, and, although this subtly altered his sound on the instrument, it still remained uniquely identifiable and uniquely expressive.

Brian Priestley

MILES DAVIS
KIND OF BLUE

3-SECOND RIFF
After the urgent complexity of bebop, the unhurried, distilled music of *Kind of Blue* inspired a new generation of listeners and players.

3-MINUTE IMPROVISATION
Kind of Blue brought a new aesthetic to jazz and opened the door to wider influences, while Bill Evans and John Coltrane went on to become the leading exponents of jazz piano and saxophone in the 1960s. Davis was to shake the tree again in 1969 when his album *In a Silent Way* introduced rock rhythms and repetitive bass lines to jazz. Meanwhile, *Kind of Blue* still speaks to successive generations and continues to sell.

By the late 1950s, the bebop revolution initiated by Charlie Parker, Dizzy Gillespie, Bud Powell, and others had gained a firm hold on jazz. Fast tempos, intricate melodies, and spiky chords were the order of the day. For Miles Davis, however—the trumpeter, protégé of Parker, and already a successful recording artist—there was a need to clear this clutter and return to the essence of jazz, melodic improvisation. For his 1959 album *Kind of Blue*, Miles and pianist Bill Evans sketched out some simple themes, asking the musicians to improvise using modes (particular scales) instead of playing over busy chord progressions. On the opening track "So What," after the double bass and piano introduction, a glorious but economical trumpet solo is followed by eloquent statements from two of the most original and influential saxophonists of the time, Cannonball Adderley and John Coltrane. The blues is present on this album, but slightly remolded, in both "Freddie Freeloader" and "All Blues." The latter features a lilting waltzlike rhythm and introductory figure from the trumpet and saxophones that recurs before and after solos. Except for the stately "Flamenco Sketches," all the tracks were recorded in a single take, a remarkable achievement that may partly explain the album's consistent atmosphere of calm, creative intent and its enduring appeal.

RELATED TOPICS
See also
BEBOP TO HARD BOP
page 40

MILES DAVIS
page 100

3-SECOND BIOGRAPHIES
JOHN COLTRANE
1926–67
Saxophonist, bandleader, and composer

JULIAN "CANNONBALL" ADDERLEY
1928–75
Alto saxophonist and bandleader

BILL EVANS
1929–80
Jazz pianist and composer

EXPERT
Charles Alexander

With Kind of Blue, *Davis rejected the bebop trend in favor of melodic improvisation.*

JOHN COLTRANE
A LOVE SUPREME

3-SECOND RIFF
Highly influential, *A Love Supreme* features four musicians at the peak of their powers, totally aligned in creative intent, delivering a message beyond the music.

3-MINUTE IMPROVISATION
A product of John Coltrane's spiritual beliefs and his immense musicality, the release of *A Love Supreme* in 1965 coincided with a period of intense social and political change in the United States alongside a creative revolution in popular music. The coherent spiritual character of this concise thirty-two minute album resonated with a much wider audience than just his committed fan base and the jazz community, while inspiring a generation of young jazz musicians to broaden their creative horizons.

Recorded in December 1964 and released on the Impulse! label in February 1965, *A Love Supreme* was a summation of John Coltrane's musical and spiritual explorations of the previous ten years. By the late 1950s, his work with Miles Davis and his own recordings had marked him out as a virtuosic tenor saxophonist, an inspired improviser, and a composer of such highly original jazz masterpieces as "Giant Steps" and "Countdown." For four years, Coltrane had worked intensively with the three musicians who feature on *A Love Supreme*: pianist McCoy Tyner, bassist Jimmy Garrison, and drummer Elvin Jones—the classic John Coltrane Quartet. At just over thirty-two minutes, the album comprises a progression of four pieces. "Acknowledgement" establishes the character of the album as a spiritual quest. Coltrane's tenor sax reshapes the four-note motif of the album title, which he later chants. "Resolution," with its descending melody, showcases the talents of Tyner, while Jones's drumming provides the restless rhythmic basis, his cymbals coloring and responding to the flow of ideas from Tyner and Coltrane's horn. "Pursuance" is faster, and Coltrane's solo gives us a sense of urgency. A reflective bass solo from Garrison sets the tone for the final piece, "Psalm," in which Coltrane's simple, calm phrases draw the album to a satisfying conclusion.

RELATED TOPICS
See also
SAXOPHONE
page 56

MILES DAVIS: KIND OF BLUE
page 102

3-SECOND BIOGRAPHIES
JOHN COLTRANE
1926–67
Saxophonist, bandleader, and composer

ELVIN JONES
1927–2004
Drummer

JIMMY GARRISON
1934–76
Bassist

MCCOY TYNER
1938–
Pianist

EXPERT
Charles Alexander

A Love Supreme *was released during a time of great social and political change.*

WEATHER REPORT
HEAVY WEATHER

RELATED TOPICS
See also
JAZZ ROCK & FUSION
page 46

BASS: DOUBLE BASS
& BASS GUITAR
page 62

3-SECOND RIFF
With their unfettered approach to composition, improvisation, and instrumental colors, Weather Report redefined the possibilities of the jazz ensemble for a generation of musicians and listeners.

3-MINUTE IMPROVISATION
The explosion of creativity in 1960s rock music paralleled the major cultural and political developments of the period and effectively became its soundtrack. By the close of that decade, however, jazz musicians had begun to blend some rock-music concepts into their music and, with Weather Report at the forefront throughout the 1970s and early 1980s, this new fusion movement revitalized jazz with fresh ideas and electronic sounds and found an eager new audience.

One of the most innovative ensembles in jazz history, Weather Report brought new sounds to jazz through the use of synthesizers and the fretless electric bass. Founded in 1970, its driving forces were pianist Joe Zawinul and saxophonist Wayne Shorter. Each brought the experience of playing in leading jazz ensembles—Shorter with Miles Davis's late-1960s band and Zawinul with Cannnoball Adderley's quintet—and both were also respected composers. Their aim was to create a fresh stream of music that drew on the language of jazz, the raw strength of rock music, the ideas of twentieth-century classical composers, and elements from world music—a movement known as "fusion." More than fifteen years after 1971, Weather Report released a series of landmark albums that documented their metamorphosis from a largely acoustic group to one whose synthesizer sounds played a quasi-orchestral role and in which funk and hip-hop were active ingredients. That their 1977 album *Heavy Weather* was their biggest commercial success was due in part to the chirpy funk of its opening track "Birdland" but also to the presence of Jaco Pastorius, the virtuosic pioneer of the fretless electric bass. Bringing a raft of fresh, expressive sounds and sure-footed rhythmic expertise, Pastorius helped transport Weather Report to the next stage of their creative journey.

3-SECOND BIOGRAPHIES
JOE ZAWINUL
1932–2007
Austrian keyboardist, bandleader, and composer

WAYNE SHORTER
1933–
American saxophonist and composer

JACO PASTORIUS
1951–87
Influential bassist and composer; fretless-electric-bass pioneer

EXPERT
Charles Alexander

Pioneers of the fusion movement, Weather Report brought a fresh sound to jazz.

MICHAEL BRECKER
MICHAEL BRECKER

MICHAEL BRECKER

Although widely acclaimed as the greatest saxophonist of his generation, Michael Brecker was already thirty-eight when he released his first solo album as a leader in 1987. Titled simply *Michael Brecker*, this return to his straight-ahead jazz roots was voted "Album of the Year" by *Downbeat* magazine. Opening with "Sea Glass," a stately jazz waltz, Brecker brings an intensity to the music which clearly inspires the rhythm section of Kenny Kirkland (piano), Charlie Haden (bass), and Jack DeJohnette (drums). Guitarist Pat Metheny contributes several melodic solos while Brecker's interest in the possibilities of the EWI wind synthesizer and its unusual sound colours help propel the groove-driven "Original Rays." Born into a musical household in 1949, Michael and his older brother Randy were introduced to jazz at an early age by their lawyer father, a capable pianist who, in Michael's words, "sued by day and swung by night." Moving to New York in 1970, Michael and trumpeter Randy formed the band Dreams. Later that decade, as The Brecker Brothers, the complex, funky melodic lines from their sax and trumpet defined a series of successful albums. In constant demand as a studio musician, Michael's emotionally charged saxophone sound and technical brilliance were to grace several hundred jazz and rock albums for over thirty years until his death in 2007.

Michael Brecker's eponymous album showcases his talents as the greatest saxophonist of his generation.

KEITH JARRETT
THE KÖLN CONCERT

3-SECOND RIFF

The Köln Concert
established Keith Jarrett's
standing as the latest in a
line of brilliant pianists to
introduce fresh musical
ideas to the piano in jazz.

**3-MINUTE
IMPROVISATION**

The Köln Concert album
of 1975 signaled a new
direction for jazz piano, one
that allowed the improviser
to bypass the limitations
of the 32-bar song form
and conventional jazz
harmonies and to dispense
with the usual bass and
drums rhythm section.
But it could also be seen
as a reaction against the
electronic keyboards and
rhythmic straitjacket of
the jazz-rock or fusion
movement inspired by
Miles Davis's 1969 album
In a Silent Way.

Organized by seventeen-year-old
Vera Brandes, this first ever jazz concert at Köln
Opera House on January 24, 1975, scheduled to
begin after the opera at 11:30 p.m., seemed to
be heading for disaster. First, the sole performer,
pianist Keith Jarrett, a former classically trained
child prodigy who had already played with Miles
Davis's band, had arrived late, exhausted, hungry,
and experiencing back pain after a tiring car
journey from Zurich with his record producer
Manfred Eicher, founder of the ECM record
label. Second, the stagehands had wheeled out
an inferior baby grand piano instead of the fine
instrument intended for the concert, an error
which could not be rectified in time. Jarrett
wanted to cancel, but Brandes persuaded him to
perform. With no preconceived idea of what he
would play when he sat down at the keyboard
that evening, Jarrett simply improvised for more
than an hour, laying down rhythmic figures and
molding melodies, one moment delicate and
reflective, the next rolling out a series of
powerful chords. This musical journey, drawing
upon the many influences he had absorbed
along the way—jazz, rock, folk, classical,
gospel, and blues—delighted the full house
of 1,400 people. The ECM recording of Jarrett's
acclaimed performance has sold more than 3.5
million copies, thereby passing into jazz history.

RELATED TOPICS

See also
JAZZ ROCK & FUSION
page 46

PIANO & KEYBOARDS
page 60

3-SECOND BIOGRAPHIES
MANFRED EICHER
1943–
German record producer and
founder of ECM Records

KEITH JARRETT
1945–
American jazz pianist,
bandleader, and composer

VERA BRANDES
1956–
Former jazz concert and
record producer; music-
therapy researcher

EXPERT
Charles Alexander

*Jarrett's improvised
concert showcased the
various musical genres
that have influenced his
piano playing.*

JAZZ & THE BLUES

12-bar form The standard length and harmonic pattern for a blues chorus. The actual chord sequence can vary from simple to complex, but the overall shape remains the same.

cross-rhythm The effect produced when two conflicting rhythms are heard together.

eighth note In jazz, by far the most common form of rhythm consists of four beats to the bar (4/4). In this case an eighth note is half a beat long. The term "eighth note" is American usage. In Great Britain the term is "quaver," so there are eight quavers to a bar in 4/4 time.

hoedown A type of American folk dance, or square dance, and the form of music associated with it.

jug band A type of band popular in traveling shows in the southern states during the early twentieth century. A large stoneware jug, of the kind used for home-brewed liquor, was employed as a bass instrument, the player buzzing with his lips into the spout, with the jug itself acting as a resonator. In this context, other unconventional instruments, such as kazoo and washboard, might also be used. Recordings survive of several jug bands, including the Dixieland Jug Blowers of Louisville, Kentucky, and Gus Cannon's Jug Stompers of Memphis, Tennessee.

key change The shifting of a tune into a different key. Bands often change key to accommodate a vocalist. Well-judged key changes can add drama to a performance, an excellent example being Ella Fitzgerald's version of "A Fine Romance," in which the key rises twice from one chorus to the next.

minstrel Now widely regarded as having been demeaning to African-American people, minstrel shows were variety performances in which performers appeared in "blackface" makeup. The material commonly consisted of sentimental songs, eccentric dancing, and comedy routines representing black people as idle and stupid. Both black and white minstrel troupes were popular in parts of the country between the end of the American Civil War and the outbreak of World War II.

plantation music Work songs, spirituals, etc., sung by workers on southern plantations.

R&B Short for "rhythm and blues," the description applied in some record catalogs to product aimed at African-American buyers. The term came to be applied to the genre of black music that preceded rock 'n' roll.

ragtime Originally "ragged time," syncopated piano music introduced in the late nineteenth century and regarded as a forerunner of jazz. Its leading figure was Scott Joplin, composer of "The Entertainer," "Maple Leaf Rag," etc. The term later came to mean any lively American popular music, such as Irving Berlin's "Alexander's Ragtime Band."

rock 'n' roll A white derivative of R&B.

swing Two meanings: 1) A style of jazz that emerged in the 1930s and is widely supposed to have been supplanted by bebop. 2) A rhythmic phenomenon, unique to jazz, arising from the tension between a steady, metric pulse and a rhythmically free melodic line. Requests for a definition of swing are often met with the variously attributed riposte, "If you have to ask what it is, you ain't got it!"

vaudeville An entertainment featuring a succession of acts—singing, dancing, comedy, and "specialities," such as contortionists, acrobats, etc. In Great Britain it was known first as "music hall" and later as "variety."

A SHARED HISTORY

The blues has been at the heart of jazz from the very beginning. The three-line, 12-bar pattern of the blues was codified in compositions such as "Dallas Blues" (1912) and the works of W. C. Handy, such as "St. Louis Blues" (1914). But the blues had been around longer than that, seldom written down but often performed. Handy claimed he first heard a blues, played by an unnamed guitarist on a Mississippi railroad station, as far back as 1903. When jazz first began to be recorded, the blues was there. One side of the Original Dixieland Jazz Band's (ODJB) historic first record in 1917 was "Livery Stable Blues." During the 1920s, when recordings spread the sound of jazz throughout the United States and overseas, they both drew from and fueled a craze for the blues. All the early black jazz bands had blues in their repertoire; some, especially in the South and Midwest, seem to have played little else. White contemporaries, such as the ODJB, were quick to absorb this new form of making music. For a soloist, the ability to play a blues with ingenuity, variety, and, above all, feeling was highly prized. Countless musicians built their fame upon a blues foundation, notably Sidney Bechet, Johnny Dodds, Jack Teagarden, Count Basie, and Louis Armstrong.

3-SECOND BIOGRAPHIES
W. C. HANDY
1873–1958
Orchestra leader and composer

SIDNEY BECHET
1897–1959
Clarinet and soprano saxophone player

LOUIS ARMSTRONG
1901–71
Cornet and trumpet player and singer

EXPERT
Tony Russell

Shellac 78rpm discs on labels, such as Victor, Columbia, Okeh, and Paramount, are known as "race records."

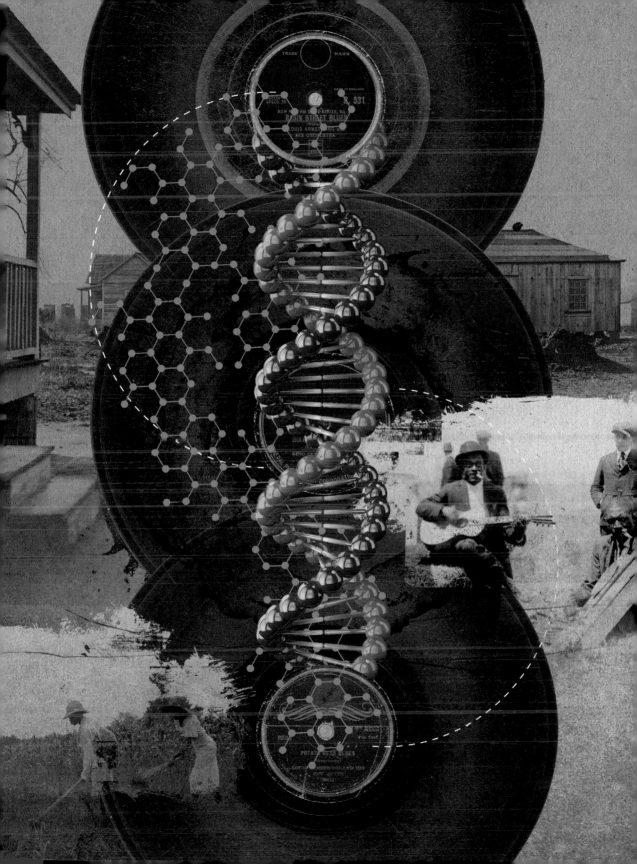

EARLY BLUES

Instrumental jazz was first recorded in the late 1910s, and vocal blues was not far behind. Mamie Smith's "Crazy Blues" was a huge hit in 1920. For a few years, the blues market was served by mostly female artists performing in vaudeville theaters and traveling tent shows. Then, in 1926, came the first best-selling blues by a man, the Texan streetsinger and guitarist Blind Lemon Jefferson. The first decade of blues on record is a cross section of African-American music, from vaudeville performers such as Mamie Smith, Alberta Hunter, or Ethel Waters, to the guitar blues of Jefferson and Lonnie Johnson and the guitar ragtime of Blind Blake. But the fabric of black music was a more intricate weave, and not all the threads were blue. African-Americans sang and played other and often older music—songs from the minstrel stage, hoedown tunes on the fiddle, possible faint survivals of their ancestral past in communal ring-shouts, and solo field hollers. Examples of this plantation music turn up in the repertoires of early recording artists such as the banjo-playing Papa Charlie Jackson and the jug bands of Louisville and Memphis, but that music of an older time became obsolete once the craze for blues took hold. What the public wanted, to borrow the title of one of the jug band tunes, was "Blues, Just Blues, That's All."

3-SECOND RIFF
What is the blues? Of many definitions, this may be the best: "The blues ain't nothin' but a good man—or woman—feelin' bad."

3-MINUTE IMPROVISATION
The subject matter of early blues was as diverse as the men and women who sang it. Many blues were—or were designed to appear to be—about everyday life as singers and listeners experienced it. Hard-times narratives of poverty and disease, joblessness and jail, the unfairness of an employer, the inconstancy of a partner. Fun-time accounts of partying, dancing, getting drunk; observations of the passing scene; sometimes even jokes.

RELATED TOPIC
See also
A SHARED HISTORY
page 116

3-SECOND BIOGRAPHIES
MAMIE SMITH
1883–1946
Vaudeville singer, dancer, pianist, and actress

BLIND LEMON JEFFERSON
1893–1929
Blues singer and guitarist

BLIND BLAKE
1896–1934
Blues and ragtime guitarist and singer

LONNIE JOHNSON
1899–1970
Blues singer, guitarist, and violinist

EXPERT
Tony Russell

Blues belongs to country and city, stage and streetcorner—to a star like Ethel Waters and to a nameless wandering songster.

JAZZ MEETS
THE BLUES

3-SECOND RIFF

Jazz and blues were a partnership in harmony: instruments followed the contours of voices, and voices took on the intonations of instruments.

3-MINUTE IMPROVISATION

One of the most iconic meetings of jazz and blues people was in November 1933, when a washed-up Bessie Smith was given the chance of a final recording session and the backing of an all-star band. Spurred by trumpeter Frankie Newton and trombonist Jack Teagarden, she rediscovered her mojo, and in the rousing party song "Gimme A Pigfoot (And a Bottle of Beer)"— which also featured Benny Goodman—she went out on a transcendent high.

Today, the phrase "blues singer" probably conjures a picture of a man with a guitar, slumped on a bed or porch, or standing at a rural crossroads waiting for a ride. This is the imagery of movies and album sleeves—blues as the music of solitary men and hoboes. Nearly a century ago, however, "blues singer" would have meant something different: an alluringly dressed chanteuse on a stage, accompanied by a jazz band. Many jazz musicians got their first experience of the profession in the pit orchestra of a musical show or revue. The blueswomen who headlined those shows, such as Bessie Smith, Ma Rainey, and Ida Cox, were supported by men like Fletcher Henderson, Clarence Williams, and "Georgia Tom" Dorsey, pianists whose talents embraced songwriting, arranging and bandleading. The records made by the blues divas are bejeweled with solos by leading brass and reeds players of the day. Cornet players Louis Armstrong and Tommy Ladnier, trombonist Charlie Green, and clarinetist Buster Bailey brought vivid lighting and dramatic staging to the compact playlet of the blues song. In their classic 1925 recording of "St. Louis Blues," Bessie Smith and Armstrong cease to be singer and accompanist and become a duet, voice and instrument combining in a performance of compelling emotional power.

RELATED TOPIC

See also
DIVAS
page 74

3-SECOND BIOGRAPHIES

MA RAINEY
1886–1939
Blues singer

CLARENCE WILLIAMS
1893–1965
Pianist, composer, and bandleader

BESSIE SMITH
1894–1937
Blues singer

EXPERT

Tony Russell

"The Empress of the Blues," Bessie Smith, brought majesty to the vaudeville stage and drama to the blues.

BIG BANDS & THE BLUES

3-SECOND RIFF
In the 1930s, Woody Herman's orchestra was billed as "The Band That Plays The Blues." If they hadn't claimed it, a dozen other bands could have.

3-MINUTE IMPROVISATION
How did a big band add color to the blues? Take Count Basie's "One O'Clock Jump" (1937). After the piano intro, Basie plays two choruses with just the rhythm section. A keychange. A sequence of soloists—tenor, trombone, another tenor (Lester Young), trumpet—while the other horns play riffs in cross-rhythms. Then a "walking" bass solo with rhythm, three seesawing choruses of reeds and brass and out. In less than three minutes.

In the 1930s and 1940s, blues was the main dish on the big-band menu. Many of the hits and signature tunes of big band jazz and swing were blues: Count Basie's "One O'Clock Jump," Woody Herman's "At The Woodchopper's Ball" and "Caldonia," Erskine Hawkins's "After Hours," Benny Goodman's "Roll 'Em" and "Sugarfoot Stomp," Lucky Millinder's "Little John Special"—the list could go on indefinitely. The first theme of Glenn Miller's famous "In The Mood" is a blues. Sometimes the band gave a setting to a featured vocalist, such as Basie's broad-in-the-beam blues singer Jimmy Rushing—"Mr. Five-By-Five"—on "Sent For You Yesterday (And Here You Come Today)." Or Walter Brown, whose jukebox hit "Confessin' The Blues" was made with Jay McShann, a bandleader based, like Basie, in Kansas City, who gave Charlie Parker his first proper job. But mostly the bands blew the blues, their arrangers pitting brass against reeds and soloist against ensemble, creating shifts of light and shade, softness and stridency, shouts and whispers, ringing endless changes on the 12-bar blues. After World War II, when the economics of live music asset-stripped the big bands, the goal was to achieve a big sound with a small team, like the effervescent Louis "Let The Good Times Roll" Jordan—which led to rhythm 'n' blues.

RELATED TOPICS
See also
BANDS, BIG & SMALL
page 14

SWING
page 36

3-SECOND BIOGRAPHIES
COUNT BASIE
1904–84
Pianist and bandleader

LOUIS JORDAN
1908–75
Alto saxophonist, bandleader, and songwriter

JAY MCSHANN
1916–2006
Pianist and bandleader

EXPERT
Tony Russell

Big bands, both black and white, rocked theaters with orchestral blues, while Louis Jordan pioneered small-group swing-blues.

1925
Born near Itta Bena,
Mississippi

1949
Releases his first records,
on the Bullet label

1950
Signs with Modern
Records of Los Angeles

1952
Tops R&B chart for
months with "Three
O'Clock Blues"

1956
Reportedly plays 342
engagements in the year

1964
Records his most famous
LP, *Live At The Regal*, for
ABC

1969
Enters pop charts with
"The Thrill Is Gone"

1988
Records "When Love
Comes To Town" with U2
at Sun Studio, Memphis

2005
Celebrates his eightieth
birthday by recording
B.B. King & Friends: 80,
a Grammy-award-winning
album of collaborations
with rock stars

2008
The B.B. King Museum
opens in Indianola,
Mississippi, near his
birthplace

2012
Plays at the White House
and is joined on "Sweet
Home Chicago" by
President Obama

2015
Dies at his home in
Las Vegas

B.B. KING

B.B. King was the best known of all blues artists and the genre's most influential figure. Few guitarists in the world of electric blues did not absorb something from him, and some learned almost everything. Never a man to be typecast, he willingly experimented in playing jazz, country music, and mainstream pop ballads. But he always came home to the blues.

As a boy, Riley B. King found a passage out of farm work by learning guitar and singing with a local gospel group. After World War II, he moved to Memphis, where he played restaurant and bar gigs and presented a record show on the local black radio station. From 1952 on, he had a succession of R&B-chart hits including "You Upset Me Baby" and "Sweet Little Angel," his soulful singing underpinned by guitar-playing that sounded relaxed and insistent at the same time.

His playing models were technically skilled guitarists who were also cool and versatile performers, men such as T-Bone Walker and Lonnie Johnson. "If T-Bone Walker had been a woman," he once said, "I would have asked him to marry me." As a singer he was honey mixed with lemon, half a crooner like Nat King Cole, half a shouter like Big Joe Turner.

Throughout the 1950s, King was a headline artist on the black touring circuit. Every year he and his band logged hundreds of gigs and drove hundreds of thousands of miles. In the 1960s, he tried to capture the growing white audience for blues, and by the end of the decade, after pop-chart success with singles pitched to this new demographic, such as "The Thrill Is Gone," he was established as "the chairman of the board of blues singers."

His world widened. There were concert tours to Japan, Australia, China, and Russia, shows in Las Vegas, concerts in prisons, movie and TV soundtracks. He became an advertising icon (Gibson guitars, Pepsi-Cola, whiskey, cigarettes) and lent his name to blues clubs. He worked less in his later years, but he continued to record, often with admiring guests, such as Stevie Wonder, Willie Nelson, Van Morrison, and U2.

Tony Russell

BOOGIE-WOOGIE

3-SECOND RIFF
Boogie-woogie began as blues piano in hyperdrive, but in the 1940s its beat infiltrated every area of popular music, from jazz to rockabilly.

3-MINUTE IMPROVISATION
Boogie-woogie is not just piano music. Jazz orchestras played boogie-woogie bass figures in the 1920s in "Tin Roof Blues." Swing-era bands rocked auditoriums with tunes such as Tommy Dorsey's "Boogie Woogie" (1938), and in the 1940s and 1950s songs such as "Cow Cow Boogie," played by small groups and big bands alike, proliferated in rhythm 'n' blues, western swing, and country music. "Hillbilly boogie" is one of the roots of rock 'n' roll.

Boogie-woogie is best known as a solo piano music using the 12-bar blues form, in which the pianist plays repeated left-hand figures in the bass, characteristically using eighth notes, against which the right hand continuously improvises in the treble. It is thought to have originated around the 1870s among African-Americans in Texas, where it continued to be played by itinerant pianists until well into the twentieth century. Pine Top Smith's "Pinetop's Boogie Woogie" (1928), a piano solo with spoken dance instructions, was the first boogie-woogie hit, followed by Montana Taylor's "Indiana Avenue Stomp" (1929), Meade Lux Lewis's "Honky Tonk Train Blues" (1930 and 1935), and other notable recordings by players in Chicago, Kansas City, and other centers. Boogie-woogie became a national phenomenon in the late 1930s when Lewis, Albert Ammons, and Pete Johnson formed the Boogie Woogie Trio and made personal appearances, broadcasts, records, and even movies. Playing singly, in duets, or as a trio, they epitomized the technical virtuosity and melodic fertility that can make boogie-woogie seem the most exhilarating of all piano music. Several generations of players have followed in their wake, the German pianist Axel Zwingenberger being the leading figure in a lively European boogie-woogie scene.

RELATED TOPICS
See also
SWING
page 36

PIANO & KEYBOARDS
page 60

3-SECOND BIOGRAPHIES
PETE JOHNSON
1904–67
Pianist

MEADE LUX LEWIS
1905–64
Pianist

ALBERT AMMONS
1907–49
Pianist

EXPERT
Tony Russell

Under the fingers of men like Pete Johnson, boogie-woogie became a defining sound of nightclub blues.

ELECTRIC GUITAR BLUES

3-SECOND RIFF

Singers playing acoustic guitars are having conversations with themselves; give them electric guitars and they become public speakers.

3-MINUTE IMPROVISATION

Early guitar amplification could be problematic—in damp conditions it was prone to cut out altogether—and many blues musicians couldn't afford top-of-the-line amps anyway, so they became used to feedback and other kinds of distortion. Some got inventive with it, such as Willie Johnson, the teeth-rattling guitarist on Howlin' Wolf's early recordings, or John Lee Hooker, who could turn the faulty-amp boogie into something approaching sonic abstraction.

Throughout the twentieth century, inventors vied to find ways of making music louder, so that it could be heard above the rising racket of everyday life. For guitarists, this was a vital quest. In the 1920s, some replaced their wooden instruments with steel-bodied "resonator" guitars, but it was only a temporary solution. Increasingly, they had to contend not only with human and industrial background noise but also with the blare of mechanical music—the jukebox. The arrival of electrically amplified guitars in the 1930s created a new kind of guitarist, who exploited not just the greater volume of the instrument, but also the distinctive tone lent by the amplifier: Charlie Christian in jazz, Eldon Shamblin and Junior Barnard in western swing, Les Paul in pop, and T-Bone Walker in blues. Gifted with a sophisticated chordal vocabulary and fleet-fingered technique, Walker was also an ultracool singer and songwriter, and in the 1950s the music he recorded on the West Coast flooded the nation and swept countless younger players along with it—notably the man who would redefine blues guitar playing for the next generation, B.B. King. Meanwhile, Muddy Waters, Elmore James, and Robert "Junior" Lockwood plugged the southern guitar styles of Charley Patton and Robert Johnson into the electrical outlets of Memphis and Chicago.

RELATED TOPICS

See also
GUITAR: ACOUSTIC
& ELECTRIC
page 68

B.B. KING
page 124

3-SECOND BIOGRAPHIES
T-BONE WALKER
1910–75
Guitarist and singer

MUDDY WATERS
1913–83
Guitarist and singer

JOHN LEE HOOKER
1917–2001
Guitarist and singer

EXPERT
Tony Russell

The mingling strains of T-Bone Walker and Charlie Christian created a new vocabulary of blues guitar playing.

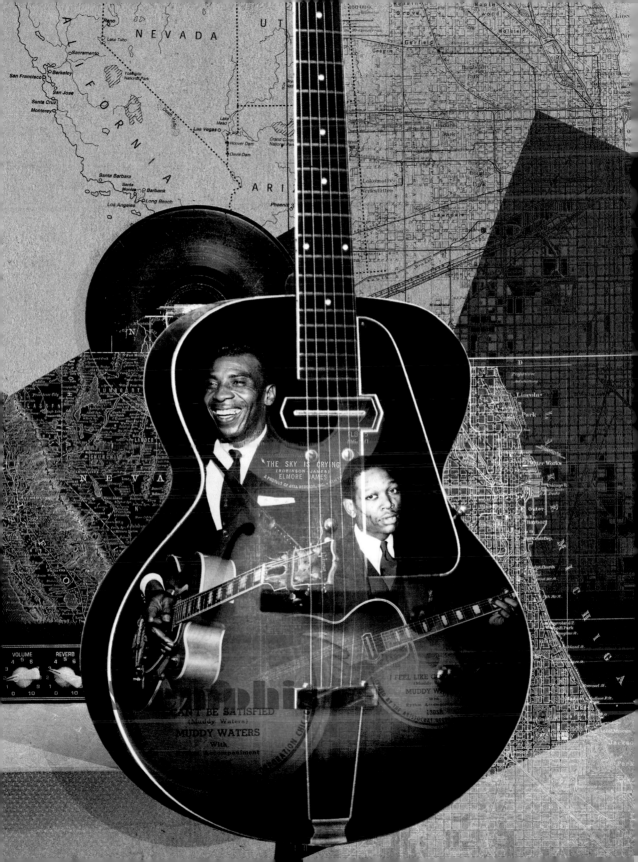

THE ROUTE TO BLUES-ROCK

3-SECOND RIFF

"The blues had a baby," sang Muddy Waters (who was in at the birth), "and they called it rock 'n' roll."

3-MINUTE IMPROVISATION

In a career spanning more than half a century, the Englishman John Mayall has taken the blues a long way, both musically and geographically. Songwriter, singer, pianist, guitarist, harmonica player, his most effective instrument has always been his band. Graduates of the Mayall academy of blues have included such major blues and blues-rock guitarists as Eric Clapton, Peter Green, Mick Taylor, Coco Montoya, and Walter Trout.

There was a fault line in urban blues in the 1940s and 1950s. On one side, the funky harmonica-and-guitar sound of Chicago; on the other, the uptown saxophone-and-piano sound of the West Coast. The Chicago blues of Muddy Waters, Howlin' Wolf, Sonny Boy Williamson, and Jimmy Reed ignited the blues boom of the 1960s and inspired groups such as the Rolling Stones and Canned Heat. In their wake, young musicians from around the world discovered the blues and formed bands. Blues became international. But some followed a different drumbeat. Alexis Korner and John Mayall, pioneers of the British blues movement, moved outward into a music that was not so much blues as bluesbased, sometimes employing jazz musicians. In the United States, Roomful of Blues recreated the little-big-band music of Louis Jordan, T-Bone Walker, and Fats Domino, a signpost toward the "swing music" craze of the late 1990s. Meanwhile, guitarists formed by blues but shaped by rock such as Johnny Winter and Stevie Ray Vaughan, became the models for a new generation of players (such as Jonny Lang, Kenny Wayne Shepherd, and Joe Bonamassa) and the unwitting architects of a new synthesis. Today, wherever you are in the world, blues generally means bluesrock: strutting guitar-hero music, blues with a dash of heavy metal.

RELATED TOPICS

See also
JAZZ ROCK & FUSION
page 46

EUROPEAN JAZZ
page 48

CITIZENS OF THE WORLD
page 136

3-SECOND BIOGRAPHIES
JOHN MAYALL
1933–
English bandleader, singer, and musician

WALTER TROUT
1951–
Guitarist and singer

STEVIE RAY VAUGHAN
1954–90
Guitarist and singer

EXPERT
Tony Russell

As blues became international, British musicians such as John Mayall and Alexis Korner, found a new slant on the blues, familiar yet individual.

TODAY IS THE QUESTION

4/4 meter Four quarter notes (or quavers) per bar, expressed as a fraction.

acoustic Literally, to do with the sense of hearing. Main uses of this adjective in jazz are: 1.) "Unamplified," referring to instruments (e.g. acoustic guitar) or unamplified music generally; 2.) Referring to the effect of the physical surroundings where music is played on the listening experience (acoustic conditions). The noun "acoustics" is applied to this whole topic.

ambient music Unobtrusive music that aims at creating an atmosphere. It relies on disembodied sound instead of structure, harmonic movement, or melody.

atonal Without any defined sense of key.

avant-garde jazz Self-consciously "ahead of its time," ultramodern, iconoclastic, cutting edge, etc. A term commonly used by jazz journalists in the 1960s and 1970s but rarely encountered now.

backbeat With heavy insistence on the second and fourth beats of the 4/4 bar.

drum & bass Form of electronic dance music, also known as "jungle," popular in the 1990s, which is characterized by fast-tempo, synthesized bass and drum patterns. It originated in Great Britain and is heavily influenced by Jamaican dub reggae.

electronica Vaguely defined genre of electronic music, influenced by bands such as Kraftwerk. Includes elements of ambient music and various dance genres.

folk music Any music originating among the people instead of from trained or sophisticated musicians. In this sense, New Orleans jazz was a form of urban folk music. Nowadays, it often refers to music in an idiom derived from defunct or dying musical traditions. The blues singer Big Bill Broonzy insisted that all music was folk music, "because it's made by folks, and I ain't heard a horse sing yet."

fusion music Any synthesis of jazz with rock, soul, funk, pop, etc.

hip-hop A manifestation of popular culture originating among African-American youth in the South Bronx, New York, during the 1970s. It consists of four main activities—rap music, creating musical patterns through the manipulation of vinyl records on turntables, extreme dancing, and graffiti. Hip-hop has grown into a full, self-defined culture and, as such, has had an influence on certain areas of jazz.

hook A catchy fragment of melody.

overdub One recording superimposed upon another.

pitch The definition of a note indicating how "high" or "low" it is. Pitch depends on the rapidity of vibrations in the air: the faster the vibrations, the higher the pitch, and vice versa. A note's vibration rate is called its "frequency."

R&B Short for "rhythm and blues," the description applied in some record catalogs to product aimed at African-American buyers. The term came to be applied to the genre of black music that preceded rock 'n' roll.

timbre Instrumental or vocal tone.

time signature The sign placed at the beginning of a piece of written music, indicating the value and number of beats per bar, expressed as a fraction.

CITIZENS OF THE WORLD

3-SECOND RIFF
Many musical cultures around the world, particularly in India and Africa, have traditions of improvisation, so it makes sense that international artists are drawn to jazz.

3-MINUTE IMPROVISATION
Although all jazz musicians are likely to reference their folk heritage, this is not the only resource at their disposal. They are also living in the Information Age and are probably influenced by all kinds of music and media, new and old. Hence the best jazz artists, from Scandinavia to Africa, play complex, multifaceted music that blends tradition and modernity.

Although born in the United States, jazz has always displayed great cultural breadth. References in song titles to Africa, the Middle East, Latin America, and the Caribbean have been numerous, and the impact of the music from these territories has been enormous. While American jazz artists have drawn on music from around the world, the traffic has also flowed in the opposite direction, and today musicians from Mauritius to Cuba to India to Europe continue to learn the language of jazz and personalize it with the rhythms, melodies, and harmonies of their own folk or classical music. The early 1990s saw the arrival in New York of a wave of brilliant young Israeli musicians spearheaded by double bass virtuoso Avishai Cohen, and their impact was considerable. Cohen's work often combines the modes and scales that are fundamental in Eastern music with a wide range of Western influences, and the results are intensely lyrical. Also noteworthy in the past few decades has been the breakthrough of several African musicians who play string instruments instead of drums. The prime example is Lionel Loueke, the inventive guitarist-vocalist who works with such legends as Herbie Hancock as well as leading his own groups.

RELATED TOPICS
See also
EUROPEAN JAZZ
page 48

TECHNOPHILES
page 140

MAVERICK ADVENTURERS
page 142

PIANO TRIO
page 148

3-SECOND BIOGRAPHIES
DUDU PUKWANA
1938–90
South African alto saxophonist greatly inspired by township song and dance

DAVID VIRELLES
1975–
Cuban pianist and composer whose music contains strong elements of African ritual and folklore

EXPERT
Kevin LeGendre

Jazz has always drawn from world music, and now, more than ever, it is a global language with numerous local accents.

BEYOND BOP

3-SECOND RIFF
Bebop, not unlike the
blues, remains something
of a core language in jazz.
It can be a stylistic point of
departure instead of an
end in itself.

**3-MINUTE
IMPROVISATION**
Today's musicians build on
the foundation of bebop in
a number of ways. The use
of electric instruments,
such as bass guitar and
keyboards, lends the music
new resonances, while the
inventive solos of pioneers
such as Charlie Parker can
act as a springboard for
entirely new compositions.
The American saxophonist
Rudresh Mahanthappa's
2014 album *Bird Calls* is
a fine example of this
lateral thinking.

Born in the mid 1940s, bebop is
an older form of jazz, but it is not an entirely
outdated one. The arrival of other schools,
such as avant-garde in the 1960s and fusion in
the 1970s, made it less fashionable, but people
never completely stopped playing it. Today,
that is still the case, and there are many young
as well as older musicians who have embraced
the genre, and in several cases they have given
the established vocabulary an invigorating twist.
For example, American trumpeter Sean Jones
can impressively negotiate the rapid-fire chord
changes and lengthy, zigzag themes that largely
define bebop, but he has brought to his work
elements of the music that he listened to while
growing up—in particular, soul artists such as
Earth, Wind & Fire. Jones's songs thus include
moments of brilliant improvisation, often at
high tempo, but he also likes to slide in funky
backbeats and short melodic hooks. Equally
important is the group The Cookers, a New York
septet that features several generations of
virtuoso musicians and plays intricate, suitelike
songs, often with a rousing gospel flavor. While
steeped in jazz history, their music is anything
but passé.

RELATED TOPICS
See also
BEBOP TO HARD BOP
page 40

PIANO TRIO
page 148

3-SECOND BIOGRAPHIES
DJANGO BATES
1960–
British pianist whose current
group Beloved grew from his
interpretation of the music of
Charlie Parker

DAVID WEISS
1964–
American trumpeter/arranger
and founder of the
contemporary bebop
supergroup The Cookers

EXPERT
Kevin LeGendre

*It may be from an
older school of jazz,
but bebop's vibrant
energy still captures
the imagination of
musicians and
audiences alike.*

TECHNOPHILES

3-SECOND RIFF
Electronics are by no
means a threat to the
integrity of the jazz
musician. They can be
highly effective if used
with imagination.

**3-MINUTE
IMPROVISATION**
Contemporary audio
software has been
embraced by many
improvisers, but they
can also produce unusual,
otherworldly sounds
without "plugging in."
Saxophonists do this by
carefully tapping the keys
of the horn while varying
their distance from the
microphone. Drummers
place all manner of objects
on the skins of their snare
or tom-toms. The result is a
very expressive kind of lo-fi
"acoustic electronica."

Improvising musicians have had
a longstanding relationship with technology—
musicians were experimenting with overdubs
and electric "varitone" saxophones back in the
1950s—and today the engagement is stronger
than ever. It is not uncommon to attend a jazz
gig and see a laptop on a piano as well as effects
pedals at the foot of a horn player or drummer.
As much as jazz hinges on the ability to play an
instrument at an extremely high technical level,
the pursuit of new sounds is also integral to the
spirit of the music, and embracing electronics
can facilitate that. American guitarist David
Fiuczynski is a prime example of man and
machine in harmony. He uses a state-of-the-
art pedal board to produce a dizzying array of
timbres, often bending pitches and
adventurously distorting phrases in a manner
that is practically orchestral. The British vocalist
Cleveland Watkiss has a looping station that
enables him to sample what he sings and then
weave together harmonies and scatted
percussion. The net result is a virtual ensemble
that can be altered according to whatever ideas
for arrangements spring to mind. Watkiss once
mimicked the sound of the wind and made an
entrancing beat from it at a London gig on
the same day that a violent storm had swept
through the city.

RELATED TOPICS
See also
ELECTRIC GUITAR BLUES
page 128

NEO-SOUL JAZZ
page 150

3-SECOND BIOGRAPHIES
HERBIE HANCOCK
1940–
American pianist, keyboardist,
and "early adopter" of
computers and audio software

CHRIS SHARKEY
1980–
British guitar virtuoso who
uses electronics with enormous
ingenuity

EXPERT
Kevin LeGendre

*Jazz musicians have
been "plugging in"
for decades, and their
relationship with the
world of technology
continues to this day,
as players use laptops
and loop stations as
they improvise.*

MAVERICK
ADVENTURERS

3-SECOND RIFF
The mavericks in jazz are unconcerned with "schools," be they mainstream or avant-garde, acoustic or electric. They go their own way, regardless of what the critical establishment may think.

3-MINUTE IMPROVISATION
So much stylistic ground has already been covered by the founding fathers of jazz that the challenge of creating something entirely new is greater than ever. Conversely, it could be argued that the richness of the roots laid down by older artists stands today's players in good stead, if they can avoid clichés. The likes of Threadgill and Coleman have succeeded in creating fresh, arresting music by way of advanced research into key musical principles, such as rhythm and harmony.

The ultimate goal of any jazz musician is to "find their own voice" and create a sound on their instrument that is original and distinctive. If they spend years working on tone or phrasing, then an individual style of writing is also at a premium, and the best jazz composers usually have a subversive streak or maverick spirit. For example, veteran saxophonist-flutist Henry Threadgill has a body of work that is difficult to pigeonhole, and he draws on virtually every chapter of the history of jazz and countless other forms of music, all the while retaining a recognizable signature. There is both a biting wit and sense of confrontation in his arrangements that reinforce their harmonic trickery. Steve Coleman, although inspired by Threadgill, has developed a different vocabulary based on highly complex approaches to meter that often draw on ancestral African, Asian, and Latin music. Coleman came to prominence in the 1980s and has had a major influence on subsequent generations of players. Several of his former sidemen, such as Robert Mitchell, Craig Taborn, and David Virelles, have matured into artists with very strong identities.

RELATED TOPICS
See also
CITIZENS OF THE WORLD
page 136

AVANT NOW
page 146

3-SECOND BIOGRAPHIES
STEVE LACY
1934–2004
Saxophonist who exclusively played soprano and developed a highly personal vocabulary on the instrument

HENRY THREADGILL
1944–
Alto saxophonist, flutist, and composer

STEVE COLEMAN
1956–
Saxophonist, composer, and bandleader

EXPERT
Kevin LeGendre

The ultimate goal of a jazz musician is to create music that is utterly personal. Mavericks, such as Steve Coleman, are hugely important.

1970
Born in Minneapolis, Minnesota

1982
Starts playing piano and is given his first synthesizer

1988
While a student at the University of Michigan he joins a band led by saxophone virtuoso James Carter

1994
Records his debut album, *Craig Taborn Trio*, with drummer Tani Tabbal and bassist Jaribu Shahid

1998
Tours and records with veteran Chicago saxophonist-composer Roscoe Mitchell

2005
Tours and records with saxophonist Chris Potter, and plays duets with fellow pianist Vijay Iyer

2011
Makes his debut for ECM records with the solo piano album *Avenging Angel*

CRAIG TABORN

Fans of both electronic dance music and jazz have long been waiting for a rightful heir to 1970s pioneers such as Herbie Hancock and Joe Zawinul, great pianists who also gleefully embraced all the latest keyboard technology. Craig Taborn carries that mantel as convincingly as anybody. Since the late 1990s, he has been using synthesizers and state-of-the-art audio software in many contexts as well as making superb albums on acoustic piano, the most adventurous of which is a trio set, 2013's *Chants* for the prestigious German label ECM.

Like all forward-thinking contemporary players, Taborn draws as much from the avant-garde as he does the swing tradition. But what sets him apart from many of his peers is an uncanny ability to elicit novel timbres from the piano and also to compose with enormous subtlety, creating entrancing atmospheres through the lingering reverberations of a single chord rather than several. Instead of making sure that every note he plays is clinically "clean" and polished, Taborn often willfully embraces the natural extraneous noise of a piano, be it the passing hiss of the pedals or roaming overtones from the keyboard, and these effects render his aesthetic all the more personal.

On occasion, he makes an acoustic piano sound like an analog synth. It is fair to argue that his immersion in the world of electronica and ambient music—Taborn has played with many of the leading producers on Detroit's techno scene, such as Carl Craig—has permeated his work in jazz. Yet the pianist is a great changeling who casts aside ready-made licks and responds creatively to each specific musical setting. Although Taborn has an impressive body of recordings under his own name, he has also been an invaluable member of many of the cutting-edge bands to emerge from New York in the last two decades, above all that led by alto saxophonist Tim Berne. Having said that, one of Taborn's most exciting recent projects is Farmers By Nature. Double bassist William Parker and drummer Gerald Cleaver are the other members of this free-improvising trio that stays true to the ideal of the jazz group that always chooses risk instead of formula.

Kevin LeGendre

AVANT-NOW

3-SECOND RIFF
Contemporary avant-garde jazz musicians make uncompromising music that challenges both audiences and critics. The best of these players are as unpredictable as they are virtuosic.

3-MINUTE IMPROVISATION
There are no absolutely clear boundaries between different schools in jazz, so the more adventurous musicians produce work that may straddle the avant-garde and the mainstream. This kind of "freebop" usually has alternations of tonal and atonal passages, as well as moments where the band plays in a set time signature and moments where it doesn't. For the most part, this music is epic and dense, but it can also be highly melodic, even lyrical.

The avant-garde movement or "free jazz" of the mid-1960s was sufficiently controversial for some critics to denounce it as "anti-jazz." Turbulent, often abrasive arrangements that were not based on conventional tonality or an easily discernible, regular pulse alienated many listeners. But others warmed to the high energy of the new music, which has endured despite the fact that many avant-garde artists enjoyed little commercial success. This may have strengthened the independent spirit of the scene, in which musicians often organize their own festivals or issue music on their own labels. Among the leading contemporary avant-garde players are the Norwegian drummer Paal Nilssen-Love and the American pianist Matthew Shipp. Each artist combines great emotional intensity and creative substance in complex, experimental work that has a fair degree of spontaneity. Generally speaking, the aforementioned and many of their peers tend to produce hard, muscular tones on their instruments—Shipp's mountainous left-hand chords and Nilssen-Love's whirlpool bass drum can shake the floor in a small club— although they do much more than create loud, at times violent, music. Their compositions are mercurial, but they also have great attention to detail and marked dynamics.

RELATED TOPICS
See also
BEYOND BOP
page 138

PIANO TRIO
page 148

3-SECOND BIOGRAPHIES
ORNETTE COLEMAN
1930–2015
Alto saxophonist, trumpeter, and violinist, one of the great founding fathers of the avant-garde

MATANA ROBERTS
1978–
Alto saxophonist, vocalist, and composer who uses spoken word and storytelling in highly original arrangements

EXPERT
Kevin LeGendre

Today's avant-garde jazz artists channel their own life experiences and cultural-political views into original music.

PIANO TRIO

There have been piano trios in jazz since the 1940s, but the last two decades have seen the format enjoy an upsurge of popularity. In the mid-1990s, Brad Mehldau and Esbjorn Svensson led groups that enjoyed great critical acclaim and commercial success in equal measure. The combination of grand piano, double bass, and drums is highly appealing, because it is a small ensemble where every note can be heard clearly when the musicians have the benefit of a sharp-eared sound engineer on stage or in the studio. Furthermore, the richness of each instrument is such that the ensemble sound can be tremendously powerful, especially when piano and bass play melodic or rhythmic lines in unison or when drums and bass strike up an eventful, playful dialogue. While contemporary piano trios may cover a Broadway standard or a piece by a great composer—Svensson made an overlooked album of Thelonious Monk's music—they often win audiences over through original tunes or inventive covers of contemporary pop artists. Above all, the piano trio is something of a common denominator between the various jazz schools. Both mainstream and avant-garde players use the format with vastly differing results. In the hands of artists who are hard to categorize—think Marc Cary or Alexander Hawkins—the piano trio is a hugely exciting vehicle.

3-SECOND RIFF
The piano trio is a classic acoustic jazz lineup that offers a wealth of stylistic possibilities. Its most flexible exponents can move from bluesy songs to free improvisation in an instant.

3-MINUTE IMPROVISATION
As the name implies, the piano trio is mostly led by a pianist. But that does not mean that the double bassist and drummer are always cast in subordinate roles. In the most creative piano trios, there is no strict hierarchy among the instruments. The double bass or drums can move center stage at any given moment in a performance while the piano plays a range of highly effective supporting parts.

RELATED TOPICS
See also
BANDS, BIG & SMALL
page 14

PIANO & KEYBOARDS
page 60

AVANT-NOW
page 146

3-SECOND BIOGRAPHIES
KEITH JARRETT
1945–
Pianist who has led the enormously influential Standards Trio for more than three decades

JASON MORAN
1975–
Pianist whose trio has both a strong blues and avant-garde sensibility

EXPERT
Kevin LeGendre

The piano-double-bass-drums format is one of the most popular lineups in jazz and offers a wealth of stylistic possibilities.

NEO-SOUL JAZZ

Jazz musicians have always listened to and played black popular music, such as R&B, soul, and funk, and eagerly drawn from its pioneers, such as James Brown. Today, that process continues, but the crucial difference is that there are several generations of improvising artists who grew up also listening to newer forms of club music, such as hip-hop and electronica. These influences have permeated the work of American musicians such as trumpeter Roy Hargrove, bassist Derrick Hodge, and pianist Robert Glasper, who has enjoyed considerable commercial success with his band Experiment. All of these musicians have worked regularly with soul singers and rappers, several of whom have returned the compliment by making guest appearances on their albums. This engagement with urban music has helped the likes of Glasper to gain access to mainstream radio and thus significantly widen his audience. A similar thing happened in Great Britain in the mid-1990s when the virtuoso saxophonist Courtney Pine brought a strong hip-hop and drum & bass flavor to his work. The reaction from pop audiences was overwhelmingly positive, resulting in healthy record sales and a Mercury Music Prize nomination for Pine's *Modern Day Jazz Stories*.

RELATED TOPICS
See also
TECHNOPHILES
page 140

PIANO TRIO
page 148

3-SECOND BIOGRAPHIES
ROY AYERS
1940–
Vibraphone player-bandleader whose funky jazz of the 1970s has hugely influenced today's hip-hop producers and soul artists

ROBERT GLASPER
1978–
Pianist, keyboard player, and producer who is the "go-to" jazz artist for soul and hip-hop audiences

EXPERT
Kevin LeGendre

Jazz's longstanding relationship with gospel, blues, soul, and funk is being farther developed by artists who also embrace newer forms of black popular music such as hip-hop and house.

APPENDICES

RESOURCES

BOOKS

All-Music Guide to Jazz
Various authors
(Backbeat Books, 2002)

The Birth of Bebop
Scott DeVeaux
(University of California Press, 1999)

The Blues: A Very Short Introduction
Elijah Wald
(Oxford University Press, 2010)

Blues People: Negro Music in White America
LeRoi Jones
(Harper Perennial, 1999)

Blutopia
Graham Lock
(Duke University Press, 2012)

The Devil's Music
Giles Oakley
(Da Capo, 1997)

Four Lives in the Bebop Business
A. B. Spellman
(Limelight, 1985)

Jazz-Rock: A History
Stuart Nicholson
(Canongate Books, 1998)

Marabi Nights: Jazz, Race and Society in Apartheid-Era South Africa
Christopher Ballantine
(University of KwaZulu-Natal Press, 2012)

Masters of Jazz Guitar
Charles Alexander
(Balafon Books, 1999)

A New History of Jazz
Alyn Shipton
(Continuum Books, 2009)

People Get Ready: The Future of Jazz is Now
Ajay Heble & Rob Wallace (Editors)
(Duke University Press, 2013)

The Rough Guide to Jazz
Ian Carr, Digby Fairweather & Brian Priestley
(Rough Guides, 1995)

The Swing Era
Gunther Schuller
(Oxford University Press, 1989)

WEBSITES

allaboutjazz.com

bluesworld.com

jazz.com

jazzcorner.com

jazzonthetube.com

jazzradio.com

pbs.org/jazz

weeniecampbell.com

FESTIVALS

North America

Chicago Jazz Festival, Illinois (August/September)
jazzinchicago.org/jazzfest

DC Jazz Festival, Washington D.C. (June)
dcjazzfest.org

Jazz in the Gardens, Florida (March)
jazzinthegardens.com

Montreal Jazz Festival, Canada (June/July)
montrealjazzfest.com

New Orleans Jazz & Heritage Festival, Louisiana (April/May)
nojazzfest.com

Rochester International Jazz Festival, New York (June)
rochesterjazz.com

Europe

Cheltenham Jazz Festival, UK (May)
cheltenhamfestivals.com/jazz/

EFG London Jazz Festival, UK (November)
efglondonjazzfestival.org.uk

JazzFest, Germany (November)
berlinerfestspiele.de

Jazz in Marciac, France (July/August)
jazzinmarciac.com/spectacles/jazz-in-marciac

Manchester Jazz Festival, UK (July/August)
manchesterjazz.com

North Sea Jazz, the Netherlands (July)
northseajazz.com

Asia

Java Jazz Festival, Indonesia (March)
javajazzfestival.com

Singapore International Jazz Festival (March)
sing-jazz.com

NOTES ON CONTRIBUTORS

EDITOR

Dave Gelly was born at the height of the swing era. He studied English and Anthropology at Cambridge University, England, where he played saxophone in the award-winning university band, the lineup for which included Art Themen and Lionel Grigson. From the mid-1960s, he co-led his own quartets and quintets with Frank Ricotti, Jeff Scott, and Barbara Thompson. He was also a member of the New Jazz Orchestra, directed by Neil Ardley. He has written extensively on jazz, and has been voted Jazz Writer of the Year. He joined the *Observer* newspaper in the UK in 1974, and has written regularly for them ever since.

CONTRIBUTORS

Charles Alexander plays and teaches jazz guitar and is also a broadcaster, publisher, jazz historian, and author. In 1994, he presented the thirteen-part series *The Guitar in Jazz* for BBC Radio 3 in the UK. His book *Masters of Jazz Guitar* was published by Balafon in 1999. The award-winning *Jazzwise* magazine, which Charles founded in 1997, remains the UK's leading jazz monthly. He is Jazz Guitar Tutor at Richmond Adult Community College, England.

Kevin LeGendre is a journalist and broadcaster with an interest in black music and literature. Since the late 1990s, he has written about soul, jazz, African-American, Caribbean, and black British authors for a wide variety of publications in the UK, including *Echoes, Jazzwise*, the *Independent*, the *Guardian*, and *Vibrations*. He has also presented programs for BBC Radio 3 and is the author of the critically acclaimed book *Soul Unsung: Reflections On The Band In Black Popular Music*.

Chris Parker began writing about jazz for *Wire* magazine in the mid-1980s, when he was the Jazz Editor for Quartet Books. Since then, he has introduced both *Jazz Today* and *Jazz in Concert* for BBC Radio 3 and written about the music for the *Independent*, the *Daily Telegraph*, and *The Times*, as well as reviews and articles for several specialty magazines, including *Jazz Review*, *BBC Music Magazine*, and *Jazz at Ronnie Scott's*. A freelance editor/proofreader, he currently writes book reviews for the London Jazz News website.

Brian Priestley is an author, journalist, and broadcaster. He has written biographies of Charlie Parker, John Coltrane, and Charles Mingus and is one of the coauthors of *The Rough Guide to Jazz*. A regular contributor to the monthly magazine *Jazzwise*, he has been heard on radio since 1971, in addition to performing regularly as a pianist.

Tony Russell writes about blues and other American music. He is the author of *The Blues: From Robert Johnson to Robert Cray* and *The Penguin Guide to Blues Recordings*, writes regularly for *Mojo* and *The Blues Magazine*, and is an obituarist for the *Guardian*. He edited the partworks *The Blues Collection* and *Jazz Greats*, and the magazines *Jazz Express* and *Jazz: The Magazine*. He has also presented radio programs on blues, jazz, and other music, and has been a consultant on BBC TV documentaries, such as *Blues America* and *Folk America*.

INDEX

ACKNOWLEDGMENTS

PICTURE CREDITS
We would like to thank the copyright owners for permission to reproduce their images. All images are courtesy of the Library of Congress, Washington D.C., and Shutterstock, apart from the following:

Cristof Berger: 49CR.
Daniele Dalledonne: 124.
DNA: 45BC.
Adrián Estévez: 49BL.
Getty Images/JP Jazz Archive/Redferns: 129CR; Graham Lowe/Redferns: 131T; Doug McKenzie/Hulton Archive: 131R; Paul Natkin: 109C; Michael Ochs Archives: 85C, 103B, 105R; Gilles Petard/Redferns: 111B, 129CL.
Glasseyes view: 144.
Roland Godefroy: 89B.
Richard Kaby: 139B.
Sheldon (Shelly) Levy: 139TL.
John D. & Catherine T. MacArthur Foundation: 143.
Mytto: 129C.
Nationaal Archief, Den Haag/Fotocollectie Anefo: 45T, 89T.
Andy Newcombe: 49CL, 49BC.
Ed Newman: 151R.
Yancho Sabev: 49TR.
Schorle: 147L.
René Speur: 45BL.
Claire Stefani: 49TC.
Suqpecoc at en.wikipedia: 49TL.
Bryan Thompson: 151L.
Allan Warren: 49C.

All reasonable efforts have been made to trace copyright holders and to obtain their permission for the use of copyright material. The publisher apologizes for any errors or omissions in the list above and will gratefully incorporate any corrections in future reprints if notified.